A DIALOGUE WITH
JOHN NORCROSS

THERAPEUTICALLY SPEAKING SERIES
Series editor: Windy Dryden

TITLES IN THE SERIES

Published titles

A DIALOGUE WITH JOHN NORCROSS
Toward Integration

WINDY DRYDEN

OPEN UNIVERSITY PRESS
Milton Keynes · Philadelphia

Open University Press
Celtic Court
22 Ballmoor
Buckingham
MK18 1XW

and
1900 Frost Road, Suite 101
Bristol, PA 19007, USA

First Published 1991

British Library Cataloguing-in-Publication Data

Dryden, Windy
   A dialogue with John Norcross: Toward integration.
   – (Therapeutically speaking)
   I. Title.   II. Series
   616.89

   ISBN 0–335–09441–4
   ISBN 0–335–09440–6 (pbk)

Library of Congress Cataloging-in-Publication Data

Dryden, Windy.
   A dialogue with John Norcross: toward integration.
      p.   cm. – (Therapeutically speaking series)
   Includes bibliographical references and index.
   ISBN 0–335–09441–4 – ISBN 0–335–09440–6 (pbk.)
   1. Norcross, John C., 1957– – Interviews.   2. Psychotherapists –
United States – Interviews.   3. Psychotherapy.   I. Norcross, John C.,
1957–   . II. Title.   III. Series.
RC339.52.N67A5.   1991
616.89'14'092 – dc20
[B]   91–17919
                                                                       CIP

Typeset by Type Study, Scarborough, North Yorkshire
Printed in Great Britain by
J. W. Arrowsmith Limited, Bristol

CONTENTS

PREFACE

The purpose of this series is to explore the ideas of established and emerging leaders in the field of psychotherapy. The interview format was chosen to give the 'feel' of an informal but disciplined discussion of each expert's ideas. It is hoped that the books convey the sense of two colleagues engaged in a searching discussion of the ideas of one of them.

The development of the books followed a standard pattern. Initially, I negotiated with the persons concerned the content of each set of interviews. The experts were given the choice of preparing as much or as little material as they wanted in advance of the interviews. Then the interviews were conducted and transcribed. Finally, both I and the interviewees went over the interviews, tidying up the English, with the latter adding or deleting material as they saw fit. In general, however each book remains faithful to the interviews as they were conducted.

Windy Dryden

INTRODUCTION

John Conner Norcross was born on 13 August 1957, in southern New Jersey, a pleasant suburban area which he adamantly distinguishes from 'the industrialized and ugly northern part of the state'. He was the second oldest of four children, all boys. He has been informed by reliable adult observers that, consistent with his ordinal position, he sought to mediate sibling disputes, perhaps foreshadowing his career as a psychotherapist and his commitment to the integration of disparate schools of thought.

His formative years are characterized as happy and unremarkable. His earliest childhood memory is playing with his brothers in the back yard. Educated at a private Lutheran elementary school, he spent his summers in Tennessee with maternal relatives and his Easters in Florida with the paternal side of the family. He survived adolescence with an intellectual predisposition and an avid interest in tennis and basketball.

Norcross undertook his undergraduate education at Rutgers University, where he received his baccalaureate *summa cum laude* in 1980 and where he received heavy doses of training in philosophy. His nascent clinical leanings were reinforced by interactions with Drs Andrew Bondy, a behaviourist, Michael Wogan, a psychodynamicist, and Winnie Lanoix, a client-centred psychologist. 'Early on,' he said, 'I learned to value the contributions of each therapeutic system and to tolerate creative tensions among them.' His early inclination for empirical research and scholarly writing were also in evidence as an undergraduate; he published several articles with both his mentors in the Psychology Department and published his undergraduate honours thesis on existential approaches to psychotherapy.

Attracted by its geographic location (the ocean), financial offer (guaranteed support) and integrative prospects (the faculty),

John Norcross pursued his doctorate in clinical psychology at the University of Rhode Island. His major professor and dissertation chair was James Prochaska, and their relationship quickly evolved from research assistant-director to collaborators, one which continues until this day. With Prochaska, Wayne Velicer and John Stevenson he initiated his influential research programmes on self-change, psychotherapy integration and clinical training. He completed his clinical internship at nearby Brown University School of Medicine in Providence, Rhode Island. Although his Brown supervisors were 'personable psychologists and active researchers', he lamented that he learned as much 'what not to do clinically as what to do' from his training experience with them.

The doctorate and two dozen publications in hand, Norcross accepted a full-time faculty position in 1985 at the University of Scranton in Pennsylvania, a medium-sized private institution in the liberal arts tradition. Why did he not select a graduate-oriented, major research university? – 'a question I have been asked dozens of times'. He cited many reasons, notably 'my love of teaching, the opportunity to balance practice and research, and to avoid the bureaucrative committee structure of research institutions'. He takes obvious pride in his students' accomplishments and revels in his role of clinical mentor and research catalyst.

Presently, at the tender age of 34, Norcross is full Professor and Chair of Psychology at the University of Scranton, and a licensed clinical psychologist in part-time independent practice. His clinical work occurs in the context of a multidisciplinary group practice which offers psychological evaluation and treatment. He joined 'a first-rate clinical operation' established by Dr Allen Duricko and, more recently, they have been joined by his university colleagues and friends, Dr Susan Williams-Quinlan and Dr Brad Alford. A short walk from his academic office, the clinical practice affords 'a great opportunity for a clinical psychologist, such as myself, who subscribes to the scientist-practitioner model'.

His five books, approximately hundred publications and editorial commitments fall into four principal areas: self-change, the person of the therapist, clinical training and, most prominently, psychotherapy integration. The natural interaction and confluence of his research interests are manifested in articles on the self-change experiences of psychotherapists, training in integrative therapy, and the synthesis of self-change and professional treatment. Norcross is editor of a Brunner/Mazel book series, associate editor of the *Journal of*

Psychotherapy Integration, former editor of the *Journal of Integrative and Eclectic Psychotherapy*, and consulting editor to several other publications.

John's personal life is, likewise, busy and rewarding. He is enriched by his 'unpredictable stepdaughter', Rebecca, his 'blue-eyed wonder of a son', Jonathan, born in 1987, and his wife, Nancy, herself a psychotherapist. 'She is the best thing that ever happened to me, trite as that may sound.' They live and play in the scenic Pocono Mountains of north-eastern Pennsylvania.

John Norcross has received numerous honours for his contributions to the field. He has served on the editorial boards of many scientific journals, and has been elected to fellowship status in several professional societies, including the International Academy of Eclectic Psychotherapists. He is listed in *Outstanding Young Men of America*, *Who's Who in the East*, and *Directory of Distinguished Americans*, among other bibliographic entries. He has been a consultant to a host of agencies, both private and public, including the National Institute of Mental Health. His first three books were taken as main selections by the Behavioral Science Book Service, and his reputation has led to offers to give addresses and workshops throughout the United States of America and abroad. Most of all, in his words, 'the greatest honour is being paid to do what I cherish – teach, research, and practise psychotherapy'.

| 1 |

PSYCHOTHERAPY
INTEGRATION

WINDY DRYDEN   John, you are well known for your contribution to what has come to be known as the psychotherapy integration movement. You edited the *Handbook of Eclectic Psychotherapy* (1986) and the *Journal of Integrative and Eclectic Psychotherapy* (1986–9). Perhaps we could start by looking at some issues of definition. How do you distinguish between integration and eclecticism?

JOHN NORCROSS   Two of our studies (Norcross and Napolitano 1986; Norcross and Prochaska 1988) and the National Institute of Mental Health workshop on research in psychotherapy integration (Wolfe and Goldfried 1988) have addressed this question. The definition of technical eclecticism parallels the dictionary meaning – choosing what is best from diverse systems, using techniques based on more than one theoretical orientation to meet the needs of the individual case. The common thread is that technical eclecticism is relatively atheoretical, pragmatic and empirical. Arnold Lazarus, the father of technical eclecticism and its most eloquent proponent, argues that we can use procedures from diverse sources without necessarily subscribing to the theories which spawned them. An eclectic can thereby minimize the impact of any epistemological and ontological incompatibilities among theories of psychotherapy.

Theoretical integration, by contrast, refers to a conceptual or theoretical scheme beyond the technical blend of methods. The creation is described as a new conceptually superior theory, a coherent and continually evolving theoretical framework. It is theoretical, idealistic and, at least for now, less empirical.

To reiterate: the primary distinction is that between empirical pragmatism and theoretical flexibility. Or to take John Davis's culinary metaphor: the eclectic selects among several dishes to constitute a meal, the integrationist creates new dishes by combining different ingredients.

I hasten to add that the goals of eclectics and integrationists are similar, although their means may diverge. In clinical practice, the distinction is largely semantic and conceptual, not particularly functional. Moreover, the two strategies are not as distinct as they may appear: no technical eclectic can disregard theory and no theoretical integrationist can ignore technique.

w.d.   Do you, John, personally favour integration or eclecticism?

j.n.   I am deeply ambivalent about theoretical integration. At this point, I describe myself as a systematic and prescriptive eclectic with future hopes of theoretical integration.

w.d.   Why are you ambivalent about theoretical integration?

j.n.   Because there are fundamental ontological and epistemological differences among the diverse therapies. Every therapy system contains a certain underlying thematic structure which embodies a way of viewing human nature, behaviour change, life's possibilities. Stan Messer's (1986; 1987) articles have been compelling in this regard.

In my *Handbook of Eclectic Psychotherapy*, which you mentioned earlier, I arranged a point–counterpoint dialogue between Stanley Messer and Edward Murray. This deep ambivalence about theoretical integration continues in my mind. It's so violent at times that it resembles a boxing match.

Let me give you a few illustrations which clearly underscore my ambivalence. I role-play the dialogue by going from one side of the room to the other when I conduct workshops on psychotherapy integration.

Round one: Messer opens by stating that clinical experience and survey findings indicate that the values of therapists are quite different. By virtue of strong allegiance to a particular way of knowing, many therapists will reject integration. Murray responds in the affirmative. Integration is not for everyone, particularly not for therapists more committed to a specific way of knowing than to effective practice. Psychotherapy integration is not for rigid, ideological clinicians who put their professional narcissism before their client's welfare.

Round two: Messer begins that clinicians do use theories and are satisfied with them. Theories, if not people, are different and have different therapeutic implications. Murray concedes the point. However, he counters that Messer is reviewing classic theories of psychotherapy, which do not exist in pure form. Psychoanalysis has become shorter, more focused, more interpersonal. Behaviourism has 'regained its mind' in the cognitive revolution. Systems theory is taking hold.

The debate can continue forever, but let me finish with one final round. You can see there is no clear victory by knockout here.

Round three: Messer agrees that minor alterations have indeed been experienced. But he repeats the essential point: there are fundamental differences between theories and between people which limit theoretical integration. Murray agrees and grants the point. When this occurs, and integrationists do admit to genuine differences, we can take several directions. Integrationists can view the theories as complementary, not as contradictory. We can use them differentially or sequentially. We can translate the processes into a common language, or we can build bridges between the two sides by recombining and reconceptualizing the theories into a new, more conceptually complex entity.

W.D.   In the next interview we shall look at your own approach to eclectic practice. It's my understanding of the field – and perhaps this is paralleled by the fact that the new Society for the Exploration of Psychotherapy Integration (SEPI) journal is called the *Journal of Psychotherapy Integration* – that theoretical integration seems to be more popular these days than technical eclecticism. Why do you think this is?

J.N.   Eclecticism has acquired an ambivalent, if not negative, connotation in many professional circles. Eclecticism has been characterized as the last refuge of mediocrity, straddling the fence with both feet planted firmly in the air, the seal of incompetency. These descriptions, however, apply to syncretism, not genuine eclecticism. So we need to make the distinction between the two, which clinicians rarely do.

Since eclecticism has acquired a negative connotation over the years, many therapists have come to prefer integration. In the United States our surveys (e.g. Norcross and Prochaska 1988) show that integration is the term preferred over eclecticism by a 2:1 margin. Another reason for the SEPI journal being called *Journal of Psychotherapy Integration* is that it represents a process flavor; psychotherapy integration as a process, not as a noun, not as a complete identity.

W.D.   Your student, Lisa Grencavage, and you (Norcross and Grencavage 1989) have written that the psychotherapy integration movement is characterized by three prominent thrusts – technical eclecticism, theoretical integration and common factors. What does your experience and research point to as the most salient commonalities?

J.N.   Mental health professionals have long observed that disparate forms of psychotherapy share common elements or core features. It may be these common elements that are the 'curative' elements – those responsible for therapeutic success, accounting for most of the gains resulting from psychological intervention. As Marv Goldfried (1980; 1982) argues, to the extent that clinicians of varying orientations are able to arrive at a common set of strategies, it is likely that what emerges will consist of robust phenomena, as they have managed to survive the distortions imposed by the therapists' varying biases.

However, the common factors posited to date have been numerous and varied; that is there is little apparent agreement on which phenomena are truly common across therapeutic schools.

Lisa and I (Grencavage and Norcross 1990) reviewed fifty published articles proposing common factors and extracted the commonalities from them – commonalities squared, so to speak, or a factor analysis of commonalities. The most consensual commonalities were the development of a therapeutic alliance, the opportunity for catharsis, the acquisition and practice of new behaviours, enhancing clients' positive expectancies, facilitative therapist qualities, and the provision of a therapeutic rationale.

W.D.   Didn't you also find something similar in your recently edited book, *Therapy Wars*?

J.N.   Yes, we analysed naturally occurring convergences and contentions in the clinical exchanges that served as the basis for *Therapy Wars: Contention and Convergence in Differing Clinical Approaches*, a book Nolan Saltzman and I (1990) edited. Thirty prominent psychotherapists of diverse orientations specified agreements and disagreements with their fellow panelists in terms of clinical formulations and treatment recommendations for the identical patient in nine cases. We wondered what content areas were most amenable to transtheoretical consensus.

The therapeutic relationship and change processes (that is, broad strategies at an intermediate level of abstraction between theory and technique) received proportionally the most consensus. Specific techniques and global theory, on the other hand, were the most frequent areas of disagreement.

Historically psychotherapy training and practice have focused on global theory and specific technique. Our results indicate, however, that these content areas are most associated with discord. If we are to search for consensus, then mid-level change processes and the therapeutic relationship would be far more productive avenues. Convergence is most probably, but not invariably, located in these areas.

w.d. What do you think is so new and important about this integration movement?

j.n. It's important, in part, precisely because it is new. A departure from the 'dogma eat dogma' atmosphere that has characterized psychotherapy for decades. The discipline suffers from sibling rivalry dating back to Freud, where therapy systems, like battling siblings, compete for attention and affection.

Mutual antipathy and exchange of puerile insults between adherents of rival persuasions have been very much the order of the day. Clinicians of disparate orientations can be blinded to alternative, and perhaps superior, conceptualizations and methods because of theoretical prejudice.

The integration movement is, to be dramatic, a metamorphosis in mental health (London 1988). Clinicians are talking to and learning from each other. This ongoing dialogue, this transtheoretical inquiry enriches clients and therapists alike. As the National Institute of Mental Health workshop put it, treatments of greater efficacy, efficiency and safety will result from efforts to integrate the best elements from different schools of therapy. Psychotherapy, a scientifically based psychotherapy, is coming of age.

w.d. Why do you think the trend towards integrating the psychotherapies is flourishing at this point in time?

j.n. The notion of integrating schools of thought has been evident in philosophy since the third century BC and in psychotherapy since Freud. But only within the last fifteen years has it become a clearly delineated area of interest. As with any complex movement, a confluence of forces has produced this recent preoccupation with integration. Let me briefly discuss five of these intertwined, mutually reinforcing factors.

The first is the proliferation of therapies. Psychotherapy systems appear and vanish with bewildering rapidity. In the late 1950s Harper (1959) identified thirty-six distinct systems of psychotherapy. By the mid-1980s (Karasu 1986), more than 400 presumably different schools of psychotherapy have been reported. The field has simply been staggered by overchoice and fragmented by future shock. Which of 400-plus therapies should be studied, taught or bought? Perry London (1988) observed that the hyperinflation of brand-name therapies has produced 'narcissistic fatigue'. There are so many brand names of psychotherapy around that no one can recognize, let alone remember, that it has become too arduous to launch still another brand.

A second factor favouring integration of late is the inadequacy of single theories. There is a growing consensus that no one approach is clinically adequate for all problems, patients and situations; we have come to demand a more flexible if not integrated perspective. Indeed, surveys of self-designated eclectic and integrative clinicians have revealed that their alignment is probably motivated by disillusionment with a single therapy system. Very few counsellors adhere tenaciously to a single therapeutic persuasion.

A third factor is the equality of outcomes. Despite a noticeable increase in the quantity and quality of psychotherapy research, it is still not possible to show that one therapeutic approach is clearly superior to another. With some exceptions, there is little compelling evidence to recommend the use of one type of treatment over another for specific problems. Meta-analytic research shows charity for all treatments and malice toward none. This has led to the equivalence paradox – no differential effectiveness despite technical diversity (cf. Stiles, Shapiro and Elliott 1986).

A fourth factor for the proliferation of the integration movement is the search for common components. This is one response to the equality of outcomes. Hans Strupp (1982; 1986), among others, has noted that significant advances in therapy research have resulted from better conceptual analyses of basis processes operating in all forms of therapy rather than from premature comparisons of techniques.

And a fifth and final reason for integrating the therapies is a matrix of socio-economic influences. The total therapy industry continues to grow: invasion of non-doctoral and non-medical counsellors, the boom in professional practice, the mushrooming of training institutes and the outpouring of third party funding (in the United States). Pressures are mounting from insurance companies, government policy-makers, consumer groups and judicial officials for accountability and co-operation.

Mental health professionals report that the impact of these

political and economic changes have led them to work harder and to adjust their treatment to the needs of their clients (Brown 1983). Inter-theoretical co-operation and a more unified psychotherapy community represent attempts to respond to these socio-political forces. Hang together or hang separately, as the saying goes.

W.D.   In my comparative chapter which I wrote for your *Handbook*, I noticed that there was little evidence that eclectic therapists were drawing on the work of one another. To what extent do you think that this is still true?

J.N.   It still has considerable validity, but less so than when you wrote it five years ago. There are now steadily emerging a series of 'second order' integrative or meta-eclectic approaches. A case in point is Larry Beutler and John Clarkin's (1990) recent book in the Brunner/Mazel Integrative Psychotherapy Book Series, which I edit. They combined at least four or five heretofore separate models of treatment, including Beutler's Systematic Eclecticism, Clarkin and Frances's Differential Therapeutics, Prochaska's Transtheoretical Therapy, and contributions from several others. Along with other contributors to the psychotherapy integration literature, they have taken to heart your observation that the nettle had not been grasped. We need to exhibit integration ourselves, not simply to proclaim it.

W.D.   I'm pleased to hear that. Is there any other evidence that members of the psychotherapy integration movement are coming together and formulating something that draws upon each other's work?

J.N.   Several examples of integrationists integrating each other's work spring to mind. One is the impressive overlap of a stage model of psychotherapy. Jim Prochaska, Bernie Beitman, Bill Pinsof, Gerald Egan and David Shapiro have all advanced similar schemes of how clients proceed through the therapeutic experience.

W.D.   Could you explain more fully to people who may not be familiar with that work?

J.N.   Certainly. In observing the complementary rather than the contradictory nature of psychotherapy systems, several clinicians have noticed that various theoretical orientations can be aligned along a temporal sequence of behaviour change. The initial stages primarily foster a working alliance, determine appropriate goals, and share the respective responsibilities of the therapist and the client. Later stages are spent explicating the historical or genetic or environmental context of the problem, raising consciousness and gathering information. Therapy then typically moves to changing the overt behavioural problem. Maintenance of that change is the next challenge and eventually termination from the therapeutic context. In the transtheoretical model, these stages are called the contemplation, action, maintenance and termination stages of change. Insight-oriented therapies (and their techniques) are most appropriate for the initial stages; action-oriented therapies are most indicated for the later stage.

Another example of the collaborative spirit in the integration movement is Arnold Lazarus' incorporation of newer proposals into his technical eclecticism, known throughout the world as multimodal therapy. He has borrowed notions from Howard, Nance and Myers's (1987) *Adaptive Counseling and Therapy*. They emphasize that clinicians tailor-make not only techniques but also relationship stances for each client.

W.D.   Now there's been a number of attempts by advocates of therapeutic schools to claim that their schools are themselves integrative. I'm thinking of three examples, I guess. One recent example would be Ellis's claim that rational-emotive therapy (RET) is in and of itself an integrative model of treatment. Second, C. H. Patterson has argued that his ideas are truly eclectic. Third, you mentioned in a recent article (Alford and Norcross 1991) that Beck's cognitive therapy may be integrative. How do you view these things?

J.N.   All therapy systems invariably, in their development, integrate what came before. Freud was an integrative therapist in a sense – experimenting with multiple techniques, discarding some, adding new methods into his therapeutic repertoire. Knowledge acquisition is an inevitable process of assimilation and accommodation, divergence and convergence, antithesis and thesis. In this light practically any therapist can, with some justification, claim to be integrative.

The essence, for me, is the process of integration. We are now witnessing integrative systems synthesizing three or more theoretical schools of psychotherapy and a multitude of technical interventions traditionally associated with those schools. They are rarely settling for combining two theories.

I wrote a lengthy rebuttal (1990) to Patterson's article (1989) published in *Psychotherapy* in which I took him to task for advocating a unitary view of human nature and for suggesting that only he had ever created an integrative product. His proposals represent regression. Although I certainly do not view his as an integrative perspective, he and others can call anything they do integrative.

Brad Alford and I (1991) have recently finished an article for the inaugural volume of the *Journal of Psychotherapy Integration* demonstrating how Beck's cognitive therapy can be considered integrative according to selected criteria. Beck embraces common factors, but obviously translates them into cognitive terms. He is technically eclectic in selection of therapeutic methods. In the development of this particular form of cognitive therapy, he also borrowed from a number of theoretical orientations, notably psychoanalysis and social learning, but evolved them in his own unique direction. I think his cognitive therapy has modest validity as a pure-form claimant for an integrative therapy.

W.D.   Over and above RET?

J.N.   Ellis's claim is highly unique because it goes back so many years and because he purports to integrate humanistic, cognitive and behavioural systems. The constituent parts of RET have been emphasized or de-emphasized over the years according to the theoretical predilections of the American scene at the time. As I read him in the 1960s, Al was far more humanistically inclined then he is now, consistent with the popularity of humanistic approaches in the 1960s. Now he largely situates or frames RET within the context of cognitive-behaviour therapy.

I think he is properly regarded as one of the earlier integrative therapists. In fact, we asked him to write an invited article (Ellis 1987) to that effect in the *Journal of Integrative and Eclectic Psychotherapy* several years ago. I would not regard him as a contemporary eclectic in that he has absolutely no use for certain systems, including psychodynamic approaches, and has become rather fixed on certain theoretical propositions.

W.D.   So in order to be currently accepted as an integrationist, are you saying that one has to draw upon all the latest editions?

J.N.   Let me clarify. To call oneself or one's work integrative is a matter of self-definition. I respect anyone who wishes to go by that moniker. However, the unofficial Norcross definition is that one must draw from at least three distinct systems of therapy or the techniques traditionally associated with them. Any three of the empirically evaluated brand-name psychotherapies on the scene today.

W.D.   Can you please name them?

J.N.   Psychodynamic, behavioural, cognitive, existential-human-
istic, client/person-centred, and family systems.

W.D.   One hope articulated by a number of people is that eventually
the integration movement will yield a language that will be
universally accepted. We will, in a sense, be united under this
comforting umbrella, presumably dancing hand in hand towards
the sunset. As you can probably tell by my language, I'm rather
sceptical about this prospect. What's your view of this aspiration?

J.N.   I am equally sceptical, at least at this point. I call it the search
for the 'holy grail'; occasionally it is known as the 'unification
movement'. A single, superordinate framework purporting to
unite all the psychotherapies is obviously ambitious and, simultaneously, probably doomed to failure because its grasp is greater
than its reach. I do not envision a universal language being
accepted at this point in the evolution of psychotherapy integration. It is premature to advance any single eclectic, integrative
or common factors approach to the exclusion of others.

My hope is that a number of sophisticated integrative systems
will be offered, each building on the other and each willing to
subject itself to the unflattering light of critical inquiry. In this
way, the evolutionary process of assimilation and accommodation
can operate. However, the eventual possession of a single unifying
theory for all psychotherapies is neither viable nor desirable in my
opinion.

W.D.   Several years ago a number of people advocated a common
language as an integrative scheme. Of course, we had a number of
people advocating different common languages, such as information processing and ordinary language. My understanding of
recent SEPI conferences is that the trend has declined. Would you
agree with that?

J.N.   As reflected in the content of the annual meetings of the Society
for the Exploration of Psychotherapy Integration (SEPI), it
certainly seems to be the case. However, there is a drive toward
common languages for specific purposes. One of those purposes,
the unifying overarching theory, has largely been abandoned. Stan
Messer (1987) called it the Tower of Babble. None the less,
common languages for more specific purposes are being advocated
and used.

W.D.   Can you give me an example of a common language for a
specific purpose?

J.N.   One purpose is to use the vernacular – ordinary, descriptive language – as a way of dialoguing across orientations. For example behaviourists and psychoanalysts do not communicate frequently because they are mutually driven off by each other's buzz words, jargon. A common language can bridge the precipice of jargon, allowing therapists to communicate and learn from each other and enrich practice (cf. Goldfried 1987).

Another common language purpose would be a research *Esperanto*, an operationalized research vocabulary which would allow researchers of different persuasions to communicate and to share their results with colleagues from different persuasions. One example of the need for this common language is that empirical research pertaining to psychoanalytic psychotherapy is published largely in psychoanalytic journals. It is absolutely unknown among proponents of most other theoretical orientations as though it never existed. If we could agree on a common language for exchanging research findings, then more progress might be forthcoming.

w.d.   What are the most common means of integration – theories, techniques, strategies, format practice, or what?

j.n.   The short and simple answer is yes to all of them and more. Clinicians are mixing and mingling techniques, theories and formats. We wondered whether members of the psychotherapy integration movement define the combination of therapy formats and the combination of medication and psychotherapy as part of the movement. In both cases, when surveyed, over 80 per cent of SEPI members considered these to be within the purview of psychotherapy integration. Of course, the addition of medication leads to integrative treatment rather than integrative psychotherapy *per se*.

These findings underscore the obvious. Psychotherapy integration comes in many guises and manifestations. It clearly is not a monolithic entity or a single operationalized system. To refer to *the* eclectic or integrative approach falls prey to the 'uniformity myth'.

w.d.   How can the average psychotherapist benefit from the integration movement? How can he or she contribute to it?

j.n.   There are a multitude of benefits, some of which we have just discussed. One will be systematic practice – systematically determining the most appropriate therapeutic interventions, making justifiable treatment selection decisions. The strengths of systematic integration lie in its ability to be taught, replicated and evaluated. Rotter (1954) years ago said that all systematic thinking involves the synthesis of pre-existing points of view. It is not a question of whether or not to be eclectic but whether to be consistent and systematic.

Another benefit will be prescriptive matching. Prescriptionism is concerned with the elusive, empirically driven match among patient, disorder, therapist and treatment (Norcross 1991). With increasing refinement in the categorization of disorders and more precise delineation of change strategies, further advantages of prescriptive treatments may be found. At that point, effective therapy will be defined not by its brand name, but by how well it meets the need of the patient.

Another advantage of integration I would like to mention is informed pluralism. Viewing disparate systems not as adversity, but as a welcome diversity. Commonalities and convergence are there, if one looks for them. Pluralism should not be equated with empty-headiness. A maharishi once put it nicely: An open mind is a good thing. But don't keep it so open that your brains fall out!

W.D.   That's all very well for the practitioner but let's look at the other side of the coin – benefits to clients. I'd like you to answer this in two ways. The first is clinically; the second is the research evidence. Is there any research evidence to indicate that integrative or eclectic approaches are more effective for clients than non-integrative or non-eclectic approaches?

J.N.   That's really the bottom line. To begin with the professed virtues of psychotherapy integration, I see three: efficacy, applicability and growth. Increased effectiveness by matching client's needs, broader applicability to client populations and problems by being more flexible, and enhanced growth of the psychotherapist by promoting relativism and continued education.

As for the second question, there is no compelling evidence that integrative therapies produce consistently superior outcomes than traditional brand-name therapies. It is important to note, however, that the converse is true as well. To date, there has not been sophisticated research that would answer the issue one way or the other to my satisfaction. That is the question has not been sufficiently addressed yet.

W.D.   Well, let's look at the research that has been done on manualized therapy, particularly the research that seems to indicate that the clinician's adherence to the manual is positively associated with positive therapy outcome.

J.N.   This is a pet peeve of mine. Not the excellent research studies to which you allude, but the interpretation of them. It has indeed been shown in at least two studies that closer adherence to a treatment manual resulted in a discernible increase in outcome. However, the implications of those studies for psychotherapy integration are not clear and are by no means convincing. The traditional limitations of this research methodology are compounded as we move into the integration area. We are talking about comparative outcome research – head to head in the 'horse-race' mentality. I do not expect integrative psychotherapy to beat, let's say Beck's cognitive therapy, in the treatment of mildly depressed outpatients. But I do expect integrative therapy to have greater applicability to a wider range of diagnostically heterogenous patients. I expect integrative therapies to be more efficient in certain cases than in other cases because of their flexibility in adopting a wide range of clinical techniques and relationship stances. If we continue to adhere to a horse-race mentality, we will never conduct research which addresses the critical questions or addresses the potential virtues of integrative therapies over pure-form therapies.

W.D.   Let us suppose that we do find that an eclectic approach does have more benefit than a pure-form approach to whatever conditions we have in the study. How can we then find out the effective ingredients given the heterogeneous qualities of integrative psychotherapy?

J.N.   When I speak about integrative therapy in this context I am referring to technically eclectic therapies. I am not speaking of an identical manualized therapy being delivered across patients and problems; rather, individually tailored psychotherapy.

W.D.   That would make it even more difficult.

J.N.   Absolutely.

W.D.   So how can we discover what in this eclectic package is responsible for success?

J.N.   The common factors and specific factors of psychotherapy are not mutually exclusive. On the contrary, I try to maximize specificity by matching technique to client need while simultaneously maximizing commonalities by establishing a therapeutic alliance, cultivating positive expectancies, and the like.

The question you raise is obviously at the core of the dismantling and cross-matching strategies in psychotherapy research. How a clinician knows what to do at any one time lies at the heart of systematic treatment selection, which I surmise we'll discuss in the next interview.

w.d. Let's have a look at some of the major obstacles to the psychotherapy integration movement.

j.n. An important question, and one I have been writing and talking about for years. The accelerated development of integrative psychotherapies has not been paralleled by serious consideration of their potential obstacles and trade-offs. Healthy maturation, be it for individuals or for movements, requires self-awareness and constructive criticism.

Bonnie Thomas and I (Norcross and Thomas 1988) conducted a survey of the Society for the Exploration of Psychotherapy Integration (SEPI) membership to explicate the pivotal obstacles. The number one rated obstruction centred around the partisan zealotry and territorial interests of 'pure-form' psychotherapists. Representative responses here were: 'egocentric, self-centred colleagues'; 'the institutionalization of schools'; and 'ideological warfare, factional rivalry'. Professional reputations are made by emphasizing the new and different, not the basic and similar. In the field of psychotherapy, as well as in other scientific disciplines, the ownership of ideas secures far too much emphasis.

Inadequate training in integrative therapy was the second-ranked impediment. Training students to competence in multiple theories and interventions is unprecedented in the history of psychotherapy. Understandable in the light of its exacting and novel nature, the acquisition of integrative perspectives has occurred quite idiosyncratically and perhaps serendipitously to date.

w.d. Any other obstacles?

j.n. Another obstacle concerns differences in ontological and epistemological issues. These entail basic and sometimes contradictory assumptions about human nature, determinants of personality development, and the origins of psychopathology, which we discussed earlier. For instance, are people innately good, evil, both, neither? Do phobias represent learned maladaptive habits, intrapsychic conflicts, or both? But it may be precisely these diverse world views that make psychotherapy integration interesting in that it brings together the individual strengths of these complementary orientations.

Insufficient research on psychotherapy integration is another impediment to psychotherapy integration. Comparative outcome research has been a limited source of direction with regard to selection of method and articulation of prescriptive guidelines. If our empirical research has little to say, and if collective clinical experience has divergent things to say, then why should we do *A*, not *B*? We may again be guided by selective perception and personal preference, a situation psychotherapy integration seeks to avoid. Encouraging empirical research on integration is now underway, but we have a long way to go.

w.d.   Given these obstacles, how hopeful are you about the future of the psychotherapy integration movement?

j.n.   I am very hopeful. In the short run, the movement has made impressive gains. To mention a few examples, eclecticism – and increasingly the preferred term 'integration' – is the modal orientation of clinicians in the United States and most other countries with which I am familiar. There are several international organizations, notably SEPI, devoted to integration. There are two or three journals and over seventy-five books that are purportedly integrative in nature.

But I have been careful of late to adopt the long view towards psychotherapy integration. There is an old Middle Eastern proverb that applies: He who plants dates does not live to eat dates. We need to be careful to plant dates rather than pumpkins. Psychotherapy integration has experienced – and will continue to experience – meaningful progress in our lifetimes. However, the greater legacy of the movement probably lies in the future. As with the clinical enterprise itself, the seeds we sow now may produce enticing flowers quickly, but may not bear the sustaining fruit for years to come. My hope, and perhaps your hope too, Windy, is that we all work diligently enough and live long enough to partake of that fruit together.

SYSTEMATIC AND PRESCRIPTIVE ECLECTICISM

WINDY DRYDEN In the second interview, John, I'd like to take a closer look at psychotherapy integration and put the focus on you as a person and as a clinician. What do you think it is about you that attracted you to the psychotherapy integration movement?

JOHN NORCROSS I can still recall the shock and dismay when I learned, as an undergraduate, that clients are frequently treated in psychotherapy in the identical manner despite their unique personalities, circumstances and problems. The emperor seemed to be quite naked. I raised my hand and asked the course instructor how this could be possible in a field I had embraced as my future profession. He shrugged, made a few lame excuses, and then cited Gordon Paul's (1967) famous research challenge: what treatment conducted by whom, is most effective for this individual with that specific problem, and under which set of circumstances. I was gravely disappointed. Early on, then, I was convinced that psychotherapists should try to tailor-make or prescriptively match therapy to their clients.

   A second professional influence was selecting the University of Rhode Island for my doctoral training. Jim Prochaska at that time had just finished an integrative book on systems of psychotherapy and was working on a major grant and a textbook, both of which were based on his transtheoretical approach.

W.D. Those are the professional reasons. What about John Norcross as a person? What is there about you that attracted you to this movement?

J.N. John Norcross as a person tends to be a pluralistic and rebellious sort. I suspect these characteristics derive partially from being raised by two independent parents and three diverse brothers. My mother was one of the first female employees of the

National Park Service at a time when it was unfashionable work for a woman, and my father was a union organizer in the south at a time when unions were unpopular organizations. Throughout my life I was socialized and reinforced for being independent, integrative, doing what was right despite orthodox. Dogma and authority were to be questioned. I bring this temperament to both personal and professional pursuits.

Malcolm Robertson (1979) has observed similar patterns – a maverick temperament to move beyond a single theoretical camp and a sceptical attitude toward the status quo – in the personal histories of other eclectics. He also noted that an obsessive-compulsive drive to pull together all the interventions of the therapeutic universe fosters the choice of eclecticism. There is some element of truth in that for me, too.

W.D.   Was your own personal therapy an influence here?

J.N.   Yes and no. Yes, in that my personal therapy was with a psychoanalytically oriented psychiatrist while I am an eclectically oriented psychologist. The occasional clash of clinicial perspectives was quite illuminating and broadened my therapeutic horizons. My personal treatment, like that of many other therapists, taught me that the human relationship is primary in therapy. But, no, in terms of any theoretical or technical direction, the importance of my personal therapy was minimal.

W.D.   Before we consider your ideas on the practice of eclectic therapy, I'd like to put something to you. You have edited two major volumes, the *Handbook of Eclectic Psychotherapy* (Norcross 1986) and *Casebook of Eclectic Psychotherapy* (Norcross 1987), and are going to edit another text, *Handbook of Psychotherapy Integration*.

J.N.   Right. With Marv Goldfield (Norcross and Goldfried, in preparation).

W.D.   You are highly regarded in the area of integrative and eclectic psychotherapy, and yet your own ideas on this topic have not been expressed very clearly. I think it could be said that you are more of a commentator on the movement than a major contributor to it. I wonder how you would react to that devil's advocate position?

J.N.   I'm not accustomed to battling with devils, but it's an observation that has been made by others, including Al Mahrer. He wants to listen to my therapy audiotapes and encourages me to write a book on the Norcross system of eclectic psychotherapy. My response generally takes several forms.

One is that what I could offer at this point in my career is a hybrid of several existing systems of eclectic psychotherapy and would not add much more than what is already in the literature. A second way of responding is that I have contributed to the empirical literature on eclectic therapy by helping to expand the transtheoretical model and by obtaining empirical substantiation for its process and outcome components. This research is in collaboration with Jim Prochaska and Carlo DiClemente.

A third way of responding is that, in an editorial capacity, I frequently wanted to put my own stamp on things. Had I promulgated my own therapy system at a relatively early point in my career, I would not have been able to accomplish the editorial work in a balanced and reasonable manner.

But I assure you: there will be a day when the super eclectic psychotherapy of John Norcross will be published in a separate book and promulgated as the greatest thing since sliced bread!

W.D.   So you concede a point on this issue.

J.N.   Yes.

W.D.   Let us move into the origins of this new Norcross development. If you were to use a label to categorize your own approach within this movement, what would it be?

J.N.   Generally speaking, I describe myself as a systematic and prescriptive eclectic with underlying theoretical predilections falling toward the interpersonal/existential side of the continuum.

W.D.   Could you outline what form this takes?

J.N.   I try to consistently employ available research, clinical experience, and common sense as the basis for therapeutic work. One of the truly embarrassing features of contemporary psychotherapy – and an indication of our relative immaturity as a profession – is that many psychotherapists treat their diverse patients with equally diverse problems in the identical manner. I am fond of repeating Abe Maslow's quip: 'If you only have a hammer you treat everything like a nail.'

The history of psychotherapy has repeatedly confirmed his observation. Sad to say, the preponderance of contemporary clinicians probably still reach for their favourite tool when confronted with a puzzling or unsettling situation. It is not uncommon for our inveterate colleagues to recommend the identical treatment – also known as their treasured proficiency – for virtually every patient who crosses their path.

As a prescriptive and systematic eclectic, I ask others and myself to become discriminating craft workers who selectively draw on experience and research to meet the multivariate challenges of clinical reality. We try to go beyond subjective preference, institutional custom and immediate availability to predicate treatment selection on patient need and comparative outcome research. That is, I try to employ and develop an expanded toolbox instead of senselessly hammering away at anything remotely similar to a nail.

w.d.   Other than a difference in theoretical leanings – he would argue that his work is social-learning and your basis is interpersonal – that description sounds quite similar to the view of Arnold Lazarus. How would you say your views differ from his?

j.n.   That's a flattering comparison; Arnie Lazarus is the father of technical eclecticism. Whether one wishes to recognize it or not, his essential philosophy is embodied in practically all eclectic perspectives. With respect to my ideas, there is also a good bit borrowed from Prochaska's (Prochaska and DiClemente 1984; 1986) transtheoretical therapy, Beutler's (1983; 1986) systematic eclecticism, and Wachtel's (1977; 1987) cyclical psychodynamics.

How would my practice diverge from multimodal therapy? Not dramatically, I suspect, but a few areas of contention between Lazarus and myself are evident. For one, I use the therapeutic alliance as a substantial process of change, more so than Arnie would. We both agree that a strong alliance is a precondition of change, of course. For another, as you mentioned, his treatment selection might lean toward social-learning and mine more toward interpersonal-existential; in particular, I am more convinced of the demonstrated efficacy of brief psychodynamic and conjoint family therapy than he is. I do not employ his modality profile and elect instead a more traditional evaluation, using the Minnesota Multiphasic Personality Inventory (MMPI). We both use his comprehensive Life History Questionnaire. A final difference that comes to mind is I am more enthusiastic about therapeutic commonalities than Arnie is.

w.d.   Let's see if we can't be a bit more specific here. Can you articulate some of the decision rules that you have in your head when you approach your clinical work? This might make some of these more generic labels come alive. What would you say are the major decision rules that you use in your work?

j.n.   I shall begin by issuing a warning I issue to the participants in my workshops: the following will be lengthy and somewhat complex. So hold on! It arises out of my firm conviction that treatment selection procedure is a step-by-step, multi-layered venture. It is not merely a matter of behavioural versus psycho-analytic or inpatient versus outpatient, but a multifaceted decision-making process all too often ignored in training and practice. We myopically focus on micromoves – reflection versus silence versus interpretation – in training. Probably more salient in determining outcome are macro-decisions and therapeutic relationship considerations.

I begin with clinical macro-decisions, drawing heavily on the pioneering work of Frances, Clarkin and Perry (1984), who operationalized these decision-making processes by providing a wealth of indications, enabling factors, and contraindications for each decision. These macro-decisions include whether to treat or not, the treatment setting, the treatment format/modality, and the possibility of adding a somatic treatment.

Once treatment setting, therapy format and possibility of somatic treatment are considered, the critical question then proceeds to: which technical interventions and relationship stances are the best match for this client's personality, disorder, situation and interpersonal style? I emphasize not only clinical techniques but also relationship stances, which is where I depart slightly from some technical eclectics. I am more impressed with the immense power and corrective experience provided by the therapeutic relationship.

In what follows I, again, forewarn people that the sheer complexities of these treatment selection processes leave one to long for the days when one would recommend the identical treatment for everyone. Unitary models of psychotherapy don't hurt the head as much even if it is like a horse racing with blinders, just running straight. The number of factors to consider in interaction with that specific client sitting across from you with these presenting problems can be overwhelming. The treatment decisions are interactive, contextual and cumulative with no main effects, only interactions. Small wonder that most mortals have assiduously avoided operationalizing these decision-making strategies.

w.d.   What client variables primarily guide you?

j.n.   Experience and research lead me to four client variables which guide my decisions. This is a manageable number for me to consider concurrently and to counterbalance; for other therapists it may be too few or too many.

The first guideline is the client's disorder, including but not restricted to a DSM-III-R diagnosis or problem list. Although we can not match with certainty, some marriages seem to work particularly well between disorder and treatment. For anxiety disorders and mild to moderate depressions the treatment of choice seems to be a cognitive therapy. With targeted behaviours, such as phobias and eating disorders, behavioural techniques are most indicated. For marital discord, of course, conjoint family systems therapy would be indicated. For chronic interpersonal difficulties, psychodynamic and insight-slanted approaches. The rule of thumb, buttressed by evidence, is that more broad band, complex symptomatologies respond better to insight, whereas more specific disorders are more amenable to action therapies.

W.D.   The second decision guideline?

J.N.   The second decision lies in treatment goals. It impresses me that different theoretical orientations probably do not dictate specific interventions to use as much as they determine therapeutic goals to pursue. Of course, the rub is in the disparate goals of psychotherapy: symptomatic, etiological or both; action, insight or both. For instance, I recently organized a panel (Norcross 1991) on the treatments of choice for simple phobia, where virtually all therapists agreed that classical psychoanalysis was contraindicated for the efficient removal of phobic behaviour. All agree, including Freud, that the treatment of choice is exposure and response prevention if the goal is alleviation of the symptoms. However, if the goal is conflict resolution and/or characterological change, then insight-oriented therapy may be the choice. It is instructive to remember differences in goals when you are discussing integration, because psychotherapists are trying to compare apples and oranges, and their conclusions wind up like fruit salad.

The third decision-making point for me is the client's stage of change, defined as readiness to overtly and covertly modify the problem behaviour. In the transtheoretical model, these stages are labelled precontemplation, contemplation, action and maintenance. Clients desiring to modify specific behaviours – those in the action stage – are best matched with behaviour and cognitive therapies. Clients desiring insight but not ready for behaviour change – those in the contemplation stage – are best served by change processes and techniques traditionally associated with insight and experiential therapies. These therapies would include Rogerian, psychodynamic and experiential.

The fourth patient dimension reflects interpersonal sensitivity –

a vulnerability to the threatened loss of interpersonal freedom. This notion of reactance is drawn directly from persuasion theory and relates to the amount of direction and confrontation that will be tolerable to a client. Clients who have both a strong need for external control and a strong perception of external influence are most amenable to therapeutic strategies that are relatively directive and confrontive and are therapist controlled. On the other hand, those clients who have strong needs both to perceive themselves as personally controlled and to resist external limitations of freedom may do best with a therapist who is relatively nondirective. Indeed these latter individuals, these highly reactant clients, may deteriorate if the therapeutic intervention robs them of interpersonal control. Larry Beutler and associates (1991) have found, and cross-culturally replicated, this pattern in several recent studies regarding reactance level.

w.d.   Before we look at a clinical vignette to demonstrate this approach in action I'm reminded of Arnie Lazarus's phrase – the 'authentic chameleon'. In order to emphasize different styles, different goals and to work within different orientations you need to be able to vary your own contribution quite widely. Do you agree with that?

j.n.   Definitely. In fact I believe this is one of the distinguishing features of a technically eclectic psychotherapist – the flexibility to render what a client needs rather than what the therapist is most accustomed to giving. That is not to say there is not a certain consistency or continuity to what I provide; the therapeutic relationship immediately comes to mind as one consistent, cross-client commonality to my clinical work. I do not think I could be relatively cold, diffident, and continually passive. Nor do I feel competent to offer classical psychoanalysis or radical behaviorism.

w.d.   There may be some instances where such an approach may be indicated.

j.n.   In those instances, I would immediately refer to a skilled clinician of that persuasion.

w.d.   One of the arguments that I have heard is that, in order to be able to move between these different styles and different approaches, one has to be a superbly trained individual who spends years here, years there. Why not approach matters differently? Why not set up a clinic where we have individuals who represent different approaches, different styles so that we can refer given patients to the person who can offer the most appropriate approach for that person's needs?

J.N.   That would be a far more efficient training procedure; however, there are a number of limitations. One is that the intake worker or the person assigning clients to the various units for services would have to be optimally trained and relatively free of biases or theoretical prejudices. Something akin to your notion does occur, one setting being the Payne Whitney Clinic in New York City, which has incoming referrals screened and then sent to specialty units including a sexual disorders clinic and a behaviour therapy unit.

Unfortunately the reality is that most clients presenting for psychological services go to establishments which have been unable to gather under one roof a comprehensive array of psychological services. Accordingly immediate availability or institutional custom, rather than client need, dictate where clients are assigned. None the less, I am in wholehearted agreement that your recommendation would work well if clients were referred for indicated treatment and if they were indeed being directed to the appropriate clinic.

W.D.   But of course, in the main, clinics seem to be staffed by people of the same theoretical persuasion.

J.N.   Like-minded individuals tend to mutually attract, which results in mental health clinics and training programmes staffed by proponents of a single tradition rather than comprehensive, integrative programmes. The cynical side of me would like one day to follow the same client into 100 training clinics with, say, a case of simple phobia, where the client expresses a goal of eliminating the phobic behaviour and has no pre-existing psychiatric history and see what is offered that patient. The cynic predicts that less than 50 per cent of the time the client would receive or would be referred to what is generally considered the treatment of choice.

W.D.   What we have then is two ways of going about prescriptive and systematic eclecticism.

J.N.   Right, one is a differential referral system, and the other is comprehensive training of the same therapist. Either the service unit or the psychotherapist can be eclectic and prescriptive. In a recent chapter on integrative training, Larry Beutler, John Clarkin and I describe both of these in some detail (Norcross, Beutler and Clarkin 1990).

W.D.   So let's take your systematic eclecticism and see how it works with a given case. Do you have a given case which would demonstrate your approach in action?

J.N.   I do. I will preface the case by saying, by its very nature, prescriptive eclecticism cannot be fully appreciated by a single case. A series of cases would be required to reflect the range of methods, formats and relationships. If it were ethically and logistically possible, I would invite you to look over my shoulder on a clinical day because the therapy I would offer will vary depending upon the needs, I hope, of the particular case.

A macroscopic survey of my part-time practice would indicate something like this breakdown: one-quarter of patients are chronic pain sufferers, treated primarily in psycho-educational group therapy from a cognitive-behavioural tradition; one-quarter conjoint marital and family therapy from a systems perspective; another one-quarter are fellow psychotherapists in individual, interpersonal-existential psychotherapy; and the remaining quarter are mixed in general.

Now, as for your question, here's a detailed example. This is the last client with whom I terminated before leaving for Europe, so I think it's fairly representative. I did not want to pre-stack the deck in either a favourable or unfavourable direction.

Let's call her Rose, a 40-ish, divorced, caucasian physician who presented with a chief complaint of panic attacks. The following synopsis is taken from my clinical notes. She was referred by a counsellor who had seen Rose three or four times and who attempted relaxation training without any discernible decrease in anxiety.

As is my custom, the client completed a life history questionnaire and a problem checklist prior to the first appointment and brought them in with her. Between the first session, in which I take a clinical history and try to establish a strong therapeutic alliance, and the second session, we arrange for some individualized psychological testing on the computer. In this case, we asked Rose to complete the Minnesota Multiphasic Personality Inventory (MMPI), the State Trait Anxiety Inventory (STAI) and the Eating Disorder Inventory (EDI).

Rose related no previous psychiatric treatment for herself, her siblings or her parents. However, she did relate a ten-year history of occasional panic attacks and generalized anxiety. She sought treatment at this time because the anxiety was now encompassing her entire life.

Developmentally she described her childhood as quite un-
happy: her father was presented as an intolerant, perfectionistic,
emotionally abusive and occasionally physically assaultive parent.
At approximately 4 years old, she experienced repeated incidents
of sexual molestation from a non-family member. At our first
meeting, she insightfully connected these belittling and rejecting
childhood experiences with her own negative introjects. She
attended Catholic schools throughout high school. After completing medical school, she transferred to a local hospital to live with a
fiancé. There are some notable fears of marriage and commitment
arising from her previous failed marriage.

Medically, Rose knew of no medical problems but she was
undergoing a comprehensive physical examination at my request to
rule out underlying organic causes for her concerns. Examination
ruled out mitrovalve prolapse, thyroid dysfunction, diabetes,
metabolism dysfunctions, and so on. She had recently begun
Xanax 0.25 mg three times a day.

W.D.   How did Rose strike you?

J.N.   Rose presented as a well-developed, blonde-haired caucasian
woman, fashionably attired. She was pleasant, verbal and responsive, although obviously quite anxious. She complained of mental
preoccupations, which were ruminations pertaining to the panic
attacks, and her intense need for controlling them.

She acknowledged a variety of depressive symptomatology: sleep
disturbance, appetite loss, concomitant weight loss, low self-
esteem, anergia, anhedonia, loss of pleasure, guilt regarding her
boyfriend, fatigue, and a mood-congruent diminution in her
short-term memory and attention span. She admitted to passive
suicide ideation but denied intention or activities in this regard.

With respect to anxiety, Rose met eleven of the twelve DSM-III-
R diagnostic criteria for panic attacks and all the criteria for a
generalized anxiety disorder. Despite the ruminations, there were
no phobias or compulsive rituals. Also, of clinical interest was a
fairly lengthy history of weight preoccupation and self-induced
vomiting dating back to adolescence. But, as is tragically the case,
she had never discussed her purging until she spoke with me.

W.D.   What were the test results?

J.N.   Her STAI showed that both her state and trait anxiety were at
the 99th percentile. That is she was clearly quite anxious now but
was clearly quite anxious even before the panic attacks. Her valid
MMPI profile showed multiple and chronic neurotic symptoms.

Depression, anxiety and nervousness dominated the clinical picture but strong obsessive features were also evident. Feelings of hopelessness, introspective rumination, intellectualization and an over-ideational approach to emotional problem-solving are characteristic of these individuals. Her scores on the depression scales were also above the 99th percentile and there was evidence of increasing social introversion of late. Also notable were clinically elevated scores on interpersonal dependency and physiological reactivity.

All the results showed that her reactance level was low. Rose was a dependent and compliant woman. This somewhat surprised me in a successful woman in the world of medicine. On the EDI, several subscales were above the 95th percentile: drive for thinness, bulimic behaviours, bodily dissatisfaction, perceived ineffectiveness, maturity fears, and interoceptive awareness. The extremely high scores on the interoceptive awareness – reflecting a lack of confidence in accurately identifying emotions or visceral sensations – confirmed the aforementioned high physiological reactivity, quite frequently found in panic disorders.

w.d.   So what were your diagnostic impressions about this woman and how did you implement treatment?

j.n.   The diagnostic impressions reached at the end of the second session were generalized anxiety with panic attacks, dysthymic disorder, bulimia and prominent dependent personality features.

When deciding on treatments of choice, I begin with the macro decisions. The indicated treatment setting is outpatient, unless no relief is obtained from the panic attacks, in which case one would consider partial hospitalization or inpatient. The therapy format will be primarily individual with occasional conjoint sessions with her fiancé. The timing or the frequency of the sessions was that she would be seen once a week, perhaps twice a week if the panic attacks continued with severity. As far as somatic treatments were concerned, I telephoned her personal physician to discuss prescribing the Xanax. Whenever I see health and medical personnel for psychotherapy, it is my standard working agreement that they should not self-prescribe but rather have one of their colleagues handle it. The Xanax was increased to 0.75 mg four times a day to alleviate the panic attacks and, with psychotherapy and the medication, they disappeared relatively quickly. An antidepressant for the dysthymia perhaps could be considered in the future but never was prescribed.

w.d. What were your decisions about the psychotherapy micro-moves?

j.n. The first decision guideline is the client's disorder. A cognitive-behavioural perspective was chosen for the panic disorder since her goal was immediate symptomatic relief which is in accord with the behavioural tradition. The cognitive-behavioural interventions selected in this case were in-office hyperventilation to demonstrate her self-arousal and production of the panic attacks, cognitive restructuring and response prevention. Since she was in the action stage of change and of a low reactance level, a directive approach, including the anti-anxiety agent and cognitive therapy, was employed. Anxiety reduction was her first priority and thus became my first priority among the extensive and historical problems she presented. We made rapid progress on the panic attacks and within four weeks or four sessions, there were no further panic attacks and have not been now for over a year.

After Rose's anxiety level was modulated, we proceeded to tackle the depression, the bulimia and the dependent personality features. Rose articulated a desire both for conflict resolution and behaviour change on these problem areas. Accordingly we selected both cognitive-behavioural and interpersonal-exploratory interventions. Here there was a rather complex interweaving, and I can't accurately trace the development. Sequentially it seems to develop naturally, depending where we are on any of these dysfunctions at any given time. We recognized the cognitive dysfunctions that produced and maintained her depression, and she particularly enjoyed David Burns's (1980) book in this area. We examined her self-loathing and disgust, arising in part from her early childhood experiences and her father's rejections. I interpreted the bulimia as an effort to both cleanse and punish herself, with which she resonated deeply. In fact, just as a psychoanalyst would predict but as I have rarely experienced in my practice, once this interpretation was offered she immediately ceased purging for the remainder of the therapy. An informal version of assertion and empowerment therapy were also introduced, and she subsequently completed an assertion training programme at a local hospital.

All told, I saw Rose over a period of thirteen months for approximately forty individual sessions and three conjoint sessions. She was weaned off the anxiolytic after three months. In her words, the 'fog was banished' and she was 'forgetting how to be anxious'. She was asymptomatic in terms of anxiety, depression and bulimia. Her termination EDI and MMPI profiles were within normal limits. She was increasingly assertive and moving forward on her life goals. She switched positions, developed friendships, decided to marry her fiancé – calling herself 'a totally different person'. Therapeutic successes such as these represent the profound joy and privilege of being a psychotherapist: to see a person grow, to actualize, to blossom.

w.d.   Can you summarize what is particularly integrative about your treatment approach to this case?

j.n.   Within the constraints of a single case, I would say there are a number of ways I could demonstrate how I am a technically eclectic therapist. In terms of theoretical orientations, directive, exploratory and experiential interventions were employed. In terms of therapy formats, both individual and conjoint couple sessions were used. In terms of somatic treatments, both pharmacotherapy and psychotherapy were used. And in terms of formal treatment and self-change, Rose's self-change efforts quickened the pace and improved the efficiency of treatment by reading books, by completing the assertion course and, of course, the homework assignments.

w.d.   Now, how much would you say your treatment decisions were influenced by hard research evidence and how much were influenced by treatment predilections and clinical hunches in this case?

j.n.   In this case, 75 per cent of the treatment selection for the panic disorder was determined by the available clinical literature, namely that the cognitive-behavioural approach is differentially effective in the alleviation of the panic itself. With regard to the depression and dependent personality, the interweaving of treatment probably represents the complex interweaving of my hunches, intuitions and the research literature. Since Rose was fairly compliant and low reactant, early on I could be relatively directive. Since it was her objective to become more independent and assertive, especially within our therapeutic relationship, I became progressively less active and directive as our relationship evolved. I wanted her to have a corrective experience, not simply an explanation, of being an autonomous agent with another health professional, a relationship she had rarely experienced previously.

w.d.   Where do your treatment predilections fit in?

j.n.   To be candid, I do not particularly enjoy doing some of the cognitive-behavioural interventions with anxiety patients. I once spent a month conducting a standard behavioural protocol for dental phobics. It was very successful in correcting the behaviour and yet I did not find it personally gratifying. To this day I refer dental phobics to another practitioner – not out of a sense of ineffectiveness but rather personal fit.

In Rose's case, I went slightly against my personal predilections in conducting the cognitive-behavioural work, but it was not such a strong resistance that I did not feel it would be successful. If I did have a strong distaste for a 'treatment of choice', then I would refer, as I do with dental phobics.

w.d.   Let's look at the human limits of integration because I think this is what we are touching on now. If we take the position that one clinician is going to be integrative, what are the human limitations that might lead him or her to referral? What are the blocks or resistances that might lead you to refer rather than offer treatment of choice?

j.n.   Yes, that touches on a key practical and training issue. No single therapist can be truly proficient in all therapeutic interventions and formats for all possible patients. Once the conceptual blinders have been removed in integrative psychotherapy, there is such a wide field of vision that grandiosity and over-inclusiveness are persistent dangers. One corrective is competency-based training, which we'll discuss in one of our later interviews.

One of the inevitable drawbacks of integrative psychotherapy training is that it will take longer to acquire competence in multiple theoretical orientations, therapy formats and various client populations. There is more to learn and thus it takes longer to learn – perhaps like bilingual students or switch-hitters in baseball who seem initially delayed in skill acquisition. It will take longer to be competent in more things. I have not yet encountered any psychotherapist genuinely proficient in all things.

w.d.   Given that, let's make this more personal. What would you say were your lacunae, personal obstacles that make you less than a supershrink, that might lead you to refer rather than accept a case?

j.n.   Lacunae in terms of time (especially in a part-time practice), competence and interest. I am not trained to conduct psychotherapy with young children, and selectively refer to colleagues in our group practice – a cognitively oriented psychotherapist, a child clinician and a neuropsychologist. Lack of competence and interest leave out inpatients with florid psychoses.

I value experience with a diversity of clients and modalities. I enjoy the challenge of dealing with patients, like those with chronic pain, with whom other clinicians feel uncomfortable. I accept them not for masochistic reasons but rather to grow as a clinician, and to accept them for who they are. When I avoid clients who are not easy, be they diagnostically complex and frustrating like a borderline personality disorder or an abrasive, non-psychologically minded man, I find that I cheat myself and that client of something.

W.D.   I'm thinking of the words of Paul Wachtel, who once said that he would be wary of a clinician who would render services to and believe that he could help everybody.

J.N.   I certainly concur. Mature clinicians recognize and accept their limitations in time, training and personality. Fortunately our practice is busy and we can refer without negative repercussions on our pocketbook. That's an ideal position for an integrative therapist who refers extensively to colleagues.

W.D.   Moving on from that point, where would you see your own professional developments coming from in the future?

J.N.   Probably in two areas. More formal and systematic training in, first, brief psychodynamic psychotherapy models and, second, in brief solution-oriented systemic work. I have conducted therapy from these perspectives and feel comfortable. However, cost containment measures in the United States will require independent practitioners to increasingly employ short-term treatments. Whether or not it is a treatment of choice, time-limited therapy will increasingly become the only treatment of the future.

| 3

THE PERSON OF THE THERAPIST

WINDY DRYDEN   In this interview, John, I'd like to focus on your interest in 'the person of the therapist'. Can we first address how the origins of your interest in this topic came about?

JOHN NORCROSS   My interest originated in the puzzlement and frustration of an undergraduate psychology student. When studying systems of psychotherapy and methods of behaviour change, I experienced a gnawing sense of incompleteness in the enterprise. Beyond the endless theories and techniques of psychotherapy, I kept asking where did the participants fit in? Why did we ignore the principal agent of change – the therapist him or herself – in course after course? How could one intelligibly learn, evaluate and practise psychotherapy while neglecting the person of the psychotherapist? In short, where was the therapist in psychotherapy?

During the 1960s and early 1970s, the person of the therapist was a popular and fruitful area of research. Then it slowly disappeared, probably owing to socio-economic pressures and to the 'tyranny of technique', as Mike Mahoney (1986) calls it.

It the last few years, however, there is a dawning recognition, really a re-awakening, that the therapist him or herself is the focal process of change. Windy, your recent book with Laurence Spurling, among two or three others, is evidence of this (Dryden and Spurling 1989). The inescapable fact of the matter is that the therapist is a person, however much he or she may strive to make himself an instrument of the patient's treatment.

W.D.   John, just what do you mean by the 'person of the therapist'?

J.N.   I mean the personal identity and professional characteristics of the therapist. Representative areas of inquiry are their families of origin, politics, values, religion, personality, interpersonal relations, coping, satisfactions, stressors and personal therapy. Of course, there are also the more professional concerns, such as career choice, training experience and theoretical orientation. I often explain my research by saying that I'm interested in the therapist as a person rather than as an independent variable.

Psychotherapists, by definition, study and modify human behaviour. That is we study other humans. The methods and principles of behaviour change are rarely brought to bear on ourselves. The reasons for the external focus are multiple and understandable. It is certainly less threatening, individually and collectively. Anna Freud once made the telling observation that becoming a psychotherapist was one of our most sophisticated defence mechanisms: granting us an aura of control and superiority, avoiding personal evaluation ourselves, and then treating others as we would like to be treated.

In any case, it seems to me that this state of affairs is backwards. The motto might be: look inward, look homeward.

w.d.   Doesn't your commitment to systematic prescriptive eclecticism, which we discussed in our last interview, seem somewhat at variance with your emphasis in this interview on the person of the therapist?

j.n.   Absolutely not. In fact, I see it the opposite way: an empirically driven, prescriptive approach to treatment selection is compatible and synergistic with an emphasis on the person of the psychotherapist. Not a dualism, not mutually exclusive, although some of my colleagues exhibit a tendency to think this way.

Multiple and converging sources of evidence indicate that the person of the therapist is inextricably intertwined with the outcome of psychotherapy. Second only to the client's history, the person of the psychotherapist is the critical determinant of psychotherapy outcome. Decades of empirical psychotherapy research have concluded that the therapists' interpersonal skills and capacity for forming meaningful therapeutic relationships account for more outcome variance than either theories or methods. Larry Beutler (1986) said that we have it all backwards – 80 to 90 per cent of the psychotherapy literature is devoted to therapy method, which accounts for only 10 to 15 per cent of the outcome variance. So, attending to the person of the therapist, not to the exclusion of method, of course, is substantiated by research.

w.d.   What kinds of qualities are we discussing? Is it more the presence of positive qualities or the absence of negative qualities that seems to be salient here?

J.N.   Both. There certainly needs to be an absence of gross psychopathology which interferes with a therapist's reality testing, energy
level and perceptual accuracy. There also needs to be a presence of
mature empathy, deep caring, mutual respect, interpersonal
commitment and so forth. As with most complex behaviours in the
world, we strive for the Aristotelian mean.

W.D.   We discussed in a previous interview the concept of the
authentic chameleon. Do therapists need interpersonal flexibility
this way?

J.N.   Yes, particularly in a prescriptive eclectic who, with one client
or in one session, might be fairly active and then become more
reflective depending upon the needs of the situation. But that is not
to say there is not some consistency there. For instance accurate
empathy, with rare exceptions, is probably a universally positive
attribute of a therapeutic relationship.

W.D.   What kind of empirical evidence do you draw upon in
emphasizing the person of the therapist?

J.N.   There are diverse sources and multiple research findings. Let
me touch on a few illustrations. One example is that a reliable, early
predictor of outcome is the nature of the therapeutic alliance
measured in the second or third session. And we certainly know
that not all therapists are equally adept at cultivating that alliance.

Another illustration is that clients uniformly rate their therapists'
caring, warmth, availability and similar characteristics as the most
important curative factors. This tends to be true regardless of the
type or format of therapy being offered; the early Sloane *et al.*
(1975) psychotherapy versus behaviour therapy study found this.

Still another illustration would be the careful examination of the
tremendous variability within treatment outcomes. Research
points to the interpersonal skills of the therapist as the prime
determinant of who does well and who does not. David Ricks's
(1974) classic supershrink study showed that it was the therapist's
interpersonal skills and personality functioning, more so than
technical competence, that exerted the impact on the outcome.

In essence, then, the value of a clinical intervention is inextricably bound to the relational context in which it is applied. I like
Hans Strupp's analogy that he uses to illustrate their inseparability.
Suppose you wanted a teenage son to clean his room. One
technique for achieving this is to establish clear standards. Fine
and dandy, but the effectiveness of this technique will vary
depending upon whether the relationship between you and the boy

is characterized by warmth and mutual respect or by anger and distrust. This is not to say that the technique is useless, merely that how well it works depends upon the relational context in which it is applied.

W.D.   You mentioned earlier that we are unbalanced in the research with the greater percentage of our research focusing on techniques whereas the greater proportion of the outcome variance seems to be accounted for by the therapeutic relationship. Why do you think this imbalance has come about in research?

J.N.   Two reasons jump out at me. If I had more time to reflect, I suspect I would come up with a few more. One reason is that some psychotherapy researchers conceptualize the therapist's contribution to treatment in a nihilistic sense. Researchers cannot systematically manipulate therapist qualities and therapeutic relationships *per se*. As a result, researchers focus on what they can control and what they know best – therapy techniques or theoretical systems.

A second reason for the relative neglect of research on the person of the therapist is one we are reluctant to admit, namely that if we are selecting people to conduct psychotherapy we should largely select them on the grounds of interpersonal skills, not their academic performance or technical competence. Again, technical competence is not irrelevant, far from it. But if someone honestly appraises the research literature and selects students accordingly, then we would modify the entire training system. The stakes are fairly dramatic; programme directors would not be recruiting students to assist in research and writing. Academic clinicians are self-perpetuating. Al Mahrer cynically concludes that most clinical psychology training programmes are for faculty, not for students.

W.D.   Moving the same subject in a different direction, you have conducted research on therapists' stresses and satisfactions. Let's take the stress side first. What are therapists most stressed about?

J.N.   It's not terribly easy to generalize about psychotherapists. A myriad of interacting variables, including professional discipline, characterological vulnerabilities, employment sites, theoretical orientations, *ad infinitum*, reciprocally determine the eventual stressors of the therapist. What I have to say is a tentative summary of my research and that of colleagues, notably Barry Farber and Jim Guy.

Probably the outstanding dimension that recurs throughout the literature is psychotherapists' personal depletion. This includes emotional and physical exhaustion, difficulty leaving psychodynamics at the office, a sense of isolation, and distancing in our own interpersonal relationships. Another cluster of stressors are those associated with the therapeutic relationship. These include assuming some responsibility for patients' lives, controlling one's emotions no matter how provoked, the strain of working with disturbed people. Another factor falls under the rubric of working conditions, and this one is particularly sensitive to organizational politics, onerous paperwork, and excessive workload.

From there, you can go on to literally a laundry list of particular stressors. These include threat of physical harm, law suits, difficulty in evaluating success, internalization of failure, and so forth.

In conducting a survey based on this scheme for your book composed of autobiographies of master therapists (Dryden and Spurling 1989), Jim Guy and I (Norcross and Guy 1989) found that prominent practitioners were just as vulnerable, if not more so, to life's exigencies as those therapists with less talent. Despite our secret fantasy that prominent therapists may have found a way to inoculate themselves against the sources of distress encountered by their patients and less experienced colleagues, a careful reading of their autobiographical chapters proves otherwise. Stress is experienced no less by our exceptional colleagues.

w.d.   I guess one of the major stressors is working with stressful clients. Can you say something about the characteristics of clients that make them particularly stressful for clinicians?

j.n.   The research in this area tends to be divided between specific client behaviours and client diagnostic types which are most stressful. In terms of specific stressful behaviours, several studies have found similar results. As experienced clinicians will not be surprised to hear, suicidal statements and gestures almost always top the stress list. Other stressors include aggression and hostility expressed toward the therapist, premature termination, agitated anxiety, and severe apathy and depression.

In terms of client diagnostic types, the most stress-inducing encounters are predictability from characterologically disordered clients, especially borderline personality disorders. Their affective and behavioural instability, intense anger, diffuse identity, self-mutilation and stormy interpersonal relationships exact an enormous toll. My clinical colleagues and I have a running gag, only half whimsical, that at any one time none of us should be seeing more than one or two patients who fall clearly into the borderline category.

w.d. That's pretty good advice. Do you find that there may be some clinicians who might find it difficult to stick to that and who may in fact be attracted to them, perhaps for narcissistic reasons?

j.n. There certainly are and I have personally met some of these clinicians. However, some people also treat an inordinate number of patients with borderline or narcissistic disturbances because they have not completed a thorough assessment and they literally don't know what they're getting into. But some clinicians are drawn for a combination of conscious and unconscious reasons to seriously disturbed patients.

w.d. What you're saying, then, is that clinicians should conduct comprehensive assessments, not only to more fully understand the client, but also to protect and forewarn themselves from excessive stress.

j.n. Yes. Several studies have demonstrated that those patients in particular exact an enormous emotional toll on the therapist and contribute more to burn-out than other types of patients.

w.d. So what can stressed clinicians do to mitigate the effects of such stress?

j.n. Despite all the burdens, psychotherapists make the best of their lot. But, as I repeatedly emphasize, we can do more than just passively adjust. We can be informed by the malaise, indeed can use it for self-renewal. We can achieve what Nietzsche liked to call great health: unhostile humour, interpersonal courage and resilience of spirit.

Perhaps most fundamental is the understanding that combating stress and pursuing self-awareness is an ongoing, continual process. Neophyte therapists in particular think that we, like the biblical Issac, can spend just one night wrestling with the angel to win the blessing. The struggle lasts a lifetime. We're not running a 100-yard dash; we're running a marathon. Psychotherapists should be comforted by the knowledge that the process, as opposed to the outcome, is the gift of self-renewal.

Having said that, there are effective means by which to reduce the inevitable stressors of psychotherapy and to prevent burn-out. Jim Prochaska and I (Norcross and Prochaska 1986a; 1986b) conducted a study on the relative effectiveness of various self-change methods to combat distress among psychologists and counsellors. The results were sensible and face-valid: use helping relationships, remind yourself of choices, and employ specific behavioural techniques – such as contingency control and counter-conditioning. All of these were positively associated with successful self-change. By contrast, wishful thinking and self-blame were negatively correlated to outcome.

External and professional measures should also be considered as means to combat occupational hazards. These could include non-vocational pursuits, such as travelling to foreign countries, and experimentation with new therapies. Herb Freudenberger, who literally coined the term 'burn-out', recommends increased private time, non-professional pursuits, better peer relations, continued training, sabbaticals, extended vacations, return to personal therapy, and transferring business details to other personnel. I also find that professional support groups or co-supervision dyads are an effective way of dealing with the occupational stress. They allow therapists to share common problems and to discuss methods to alleviate stress.

In short, care-takers should acknowledge and take better care of their own emotional needs. We – and our clients – deserve no less.

w.d. Let me pick up on one of those specific methods and look at some cultural differences that I see between American and British counsellors. In Britain, the British Association for Counselling has an accredited practitioner scheme which is renewable every five years. As you know, we don't yet have licensing in Britain, but I think we are moving towards that. A mandatory activity of accredited counsellors is supervision. It is my understanding of the American scene that supervision isn't regarded as a mandatory activity of therapists and counsellors. Is that correct?

j.n. No, supervision is required for licensure. Psychologists, psychiatrists and social workers are required to seek continued education but there is no requirement for formal supervision after licensure/certification.

w.d. Do you think that it's a good policy, or would you like to see all therapists be mandated to receive ongoing supervision?

j.n. I like the idea of continuing education and training in the broad sense and for most people that would entail supervision. I suppose I would stop short of absolutely requiring supervision, though I would add a provision that conventional supervision could substitute for pre-packaged continued education programmes.

For myself, I meet weekly with one of my clinical colleagues for peer supervision and case discussion. I find this process to be very rewarding, stress relieving, and I would certainly continue to do it whether it was mandated or not. Responsible psychotherapists, in my experience, tend to do in advance what licensure laws would have them do in the future.

W.D.   Let's look at the satisfactions. From your research, what are the most prized satisfactions that clinicians get out of clinical work?

J.N.   Psychotherapy, whatever else it may be, is undeniably intense. The intensity and intimacy are recurring satisfactions. The down side is that ordinary life and personal relationships can become anti-climactic. They don't seem to have the richness and the discovery of the therapeutic relationship.

Topping the list of therapists' satisfactions is promoting growth — that of clients and ourselves, self-knowledge, self-growth, enhancing growth, watching people being psychologically reborn. Another satisfaction would be intimate involvement, learning about many types of people, achieving one form of intimacy, being socially useful.

Other satisfactions that usually make the top ten are a sense of social recognition, of being a socially sanctioned healer, a modicum of financial success, professional independence (depending on where one works), creativity, expressing oneself, and continual growth.

One satisfaction for me is rarely recognized in the literature: the diversity and synergy of professional activities. As a clinical psychologist whose principal employment is in academia, I have combined a clinical practice with an academic career. So I teach, supervise, write, research, edit, administer (the latter rather reluctantly), and on and on. But it does raise the fascinating paradox that one of the gratifications of psychotherapy is not having to do it full-time. Do you find that?

W.D.   Yes, I do. I think that one of the major ways I manage stress is to have a healthy diversity of activities. I would find it personally very difficult to do full-time clinical work. I really marvel at people, like Albert Ellis, who seem to have a clinical caseload that would make lesser therapists groan under the strain. That brings me to an issue that we haven't touched on and that is individual differences among psychotherapists in how hardy or resilient they are. There seems to be a great variation.

J.N.   There has not been much direct research on therapist hardiness, but there are several hints. One is that people with doctoral degrees in the mental health professions tend to be more hardy and expect more stress. This finding may be a result of a self-selection process and the rigours of getting through doctoral programmes. I joke that after getting through my graduate career anything else seems relatively easy, almost pales by comparison to the number of hours worked during graduate school.

There are also differences attributable to what else is happening in a therapist's life. What else is extracting an adjustive demand on the therapist beyond occupational stress? Therapists with very demanding and unrewarding extra-therapy lives tend, of course, to have more difficulty. They may be equally hardy but cannot devote proportionally as much psychological resources to their therapeutic endeavours. I noticed that most successful therapists, dating back to Freud, have organized their lives, and perhaps their spouses, so that when they're done clinically or academically, they can return home and experience a rich interpersonal relationship and family life while not having to expend excessive energy to maintain it. I know my own wife has been instrumental in doing that for me. Although she is a psychotherapist herself, we've been fortunate in arranging our lives so that neither of us have to spend inordinate time attending to mundane household chores, and we can concentrate the time we have on each other, our family, our friends.

W.D.   You mentioned that your wife is also in the field. Is there any evidence to show that having one's spouse or partner involved in the same field can also be a health benefit?

J.N.   To be honest, I know of no specific studies on that issue. Speaking from personal experience, a spouse in the same field can be a double-edged sword. There is a built-in peer supervision that, if there are difficulties at work, the partners can discuss it. At the same time, there is a persistent danger of bringing the office and psychodynamics home, perhaps more so than is in one's best interest.

W.D.   Let's review some folklore on the person of the therapist and do so from the point of research reviews that you have conducted. I think a major one is that most therapists hail from disturbed families of origin. Is that true?

J.N.   No. Many colleagues, however, continue to insist that psychotherapists routinely come from disrupted families, often with parents or siblings who have been mentally disordered. Therapists will still encounter extremist statements in the literature based on, or perhaps I should say projected from, personal and unrepresentative experiences. Just recently, someone brought to my attention this absolutist statement: 'No psychotherapist I have known came out of happy, comfortable years'.

And yet the best systematic research we have, such as that of Henry, Sims and Spray (1971; 1973), refutes the notion that therapists derive from families with a higher rate of mental disorder. Their overall conclusion regarding families of origin is normalcy; the occurrence of mental illness in the therapist's family is similar to that experienced by members of the general population. While the vocational choice of a minority of psychotherapists has probably been strongly influenced by early personal experiences with emotionally disturbed people, that does not appear to be true of most clinicians.

Much of the folklore is, in actuality, archaic stereotypes. Half-truths and misconceptions abound in our discipline. Families are not alone in shared myths; professions, consciously and unconsciously, collude in maintaining them.

A few years ago, for another example, my wife enrolled in a graduate-level psychopathology course. The instructor, an otherwise affable and educated social worker, asked the class if anyone knew what psychologists did 'besides testing', since he didn't. This ignorant slander would be akin to enquiring what social workers do besides distributing welfare cheques or what psychiatrists do besides pushing drugs.

These myths are partly the product of innocent ignorance, uninformed opinion. I can accept them when they are relatively amenable to ratiocination, but they are also partly prejudice – wilful ignorance, fanned by turf wars, separation of the various mental health professionals, and paucity of reliable information on the person of the therapist. My current writing project, a book on the person of the psychotherapist, provides a concise refutation of these misleading folklore. They damage the profession, the reputation of therapists and, perhaps most distressingly, prevent people from seeking our services.

w.d.   Let's look at one or two more myths if we might. One view, which I think is held quite widely by trainers, is that it would be better for students to experience psychological distress or have been exposed to such distress in either their family of origin or in their interpersonal relationships. Is this is a myth?

j.n.   Not a myth, but taken to extremes, it can be both illogical and harmful. Albert Schweitzer said that having experienced and known the pain, we are better able to recognize and treat it in other people. I believe this to be the case, particularly in development of an empathic capacity and the ability to resonate with another person's inner turmoil. However, taken to extreme, this policy would have that only schizophrenics should treat schizophrenics and that only recovering alcoholics should treat alcoholics. The latter has become a far too common reality in the United States with damaging implications for the field. It takes on an anti-scientific edge to it: 'I know what worked for me. Let me impose that on you. Damn the research literature.' This is a dangerous and, under certain circumstances, an unethical perspective.

I would like psychotherapy students to have encountered psychological obstacles themselves, to be acquainted with pain, not to always have had an emotional silver spoon in their mouths. On the other hand, I trust trainees are not clinically disturbed and do not rigidly impose the treatment that worked for them on to their clients.

W.D.   Let's consider the notion that therapists are either crazy or wounded in some way, the concept of the wounded healer. To what extent is that true?

J.N.   The mythological image of the wounded healer is widespread. Primitive shamans, for instance, had a mixture of both priestly and healing powers. A requirement for the role was that they possess some defect, which in our largely western society has been recognised as an illness or disability.

There are many other examples of the wounded healer. In the highest sense, Jesus Christ was a wounded healer. He is the psychological symbol for all sins and was destined to die while, at the same time, healed the world and offered external redemption.

Many psychotherapists, I believe, enter the profession partly due to this affinity to heal the patient archetype. Practitioners, medical and psychological alike, are accused (and occasionally accurately) of being more interested in pathology than health, more interested in abnormality than normality. This is half true. Psychotherapists are attracted to this health–sickness polarity not as end in itself. The image of the wounded healer symbolizes a painful awareness of our own limitations and the counterpole to health.

In your book with Laurence Spurling, *On Becoming a Psychotherapist*, the majority of your ten contributors alluded to early personal vulnerabilities, which predisposed them to careers as psychotherapists. However, only one explicitly referred to the 'wounded healer'. The incidence of this dynamic constellation in psychotherapists is much greater than commonly recognized in your book and elsewhere. Moreover, it can be – and probably should be – fruitfully considered by each person.

I am careful to distinguish between the wounded healer and the unproductive psychopathology of the therapist. The former is a personal predilection, an early vulnerability that makes one more sensitive to distress, pain and exclusion, while the latter is disruptive and makes one insensitive because of internal demands.

In my own history, an example of the wounded healer is that I had a minor speech impediment. My mother took me to a speech therapist for a few months, a pleasant man who made me do incredibly difficult things with my tongue. In retrospect, though he was perhaps not a healer in the traditional sense, the experience was liberating in that it was painful and embarrassing not to be able to express myself as I would like.

w.d.   I can resonate to what you just said because when I was much younger, I used to have a very, very bad stammer. My experience was of being teased quite severely at school, the result of which I experienced a fair degree of personal pain which, really as I have phrased it, acquainted me with my own inner responses and got me used to dealing with feelings. Were there any elements of that experience for you, too?

j.n.   There was some teasing, but it was rather mild and in a brotherly sort of way. I do remember some pain with references to baby talk because speech clarity was the problem in my case. More so than that I recall the experience of frustration. I was fairly bright and intensely curious, and it was frustrating not to be able to express my wishes and responses the way I wanted to. Upon learning of this personal anecdote, a few of my students have immediately related it not only to the wounded healer, but also to Adler's notion of organ inferiority. The speech-impaired youngster grows up to be a university professor!

THEORETICAL
ORIENTATION

WINDY DRYDEN   In this interview, we shall focus on theoretical orientations. First, can you define the term?

JOHN NORCROSS   I'm glad you asked. Without a working definition of theoretical orientations, we would probably be embroiled in semantics all afternoon. Let me offer a definition which I published (Norcross 1985) a few years ago. A theoretical orientation is a consistent theory of human behaviour, mental disorder, psychotherapy and the mechanisms of therapeutic change. These appear to be the necessary conditions of an orientation. Theories of human development and personality *per se* are desirable, but not characteristic of all orientations, particularly the eclectic and integrative varieties.

It should also be noted that therapy is inevitably guided by theory at *some* level, perhaps imperceptible to the therapist. At times, it is reasonable to assume that formal theories may not totally capture 'theories-in-use'. In the constant interaction between the theoretical orientation and the human clinician, theories-in-use may contain a well-articulated series of gradually modifying hypotheses and sometimes a bunch of more-or-less beliefs.

W.D.   What are the uses and also the misuses of theoretical orientations?

J.N.   In the context of this definition, theoretical orientations serve many useful and probably necessary functions. Without a guiding and grounding theory, clinicians become vulnerable, direction-less zombies bombarded with millions of pieces of information and impressions. (Parenthetically this is a persistent danger of an unsystematic eclecticism). A theoretical orientation limits information, prioritizes and organizes data, describes the phenomena, generates hypotheses and directions, then integrates them all into a unified, coherent body of knowledge. They serve, *in toto*, descriptive, explanatory, developmental and generative functions in clinical work.

W.D.   Those are the uses. How about the misuses?

J.N.   There's a dark side to practically every phenomenon. Insularity and rigidity of theories are probably the greatest misuses. Clinicians can become so enamoured and attached to their theoretical orientation that they, literally and figuratively, become blind to alternative conceptualizations and potentially superior methods. In these instances, psychotherapeutic practice becomes analogous to the Procrustean bed. That is we shorten or stretch clients to fit our theories rather than tailoring our approach to fit client needs.

Another misuse of theoretical orientations occurs when they are equated with facts. Theories, we should remind ourselves, are provisional attempts to explain complex phenomena, and should not be, as is the tendency, presented as scientific facts. Orientations must be interpreted cautiously and in relation to the myriad of factors which determine clinical practice.

W.D.   From the studies that you've done, what are the most common orientations among American and British clinical psychologists?

J.N.   The general division of theoretical orientations in the United States is approximately one-quarter psychodynamic, psychoanalytic and Neo-Freudian; one-quarter in behavioural, cognitive and cognitive-behavioural orientations; another one-quarter eclectic or integrative; and the remaining one-quarter a combination of humanistic, family systems and other theoretical orientations.

Theoretical allegiance, like personal identity, is defined not only by the 'me' but also by the 'not me'. For this reason, we have assessed theoretical orientations *least* like the clinician's own approach. Overall, psychoanalytic and humanistic persuasions were tied with about one-quarter apiece as least like one's favoured orientation, followed closely behind by behavioural. These top three on the 'unlike me' list, not coincidentally, represent the traditional three schools of psychotherapy. It might be a bit self-serving, but I would note that eclecticism solicited the fewest nominations as the orientations least like one's own.

With regard to your side of the Atlantic, Windy, I am not aware of any reliable indicators of theoretical orientations. But within the next couple of months the results of our ongoing survey of clinical members of the British Psychological Society will be available and we can look at those findings.

w.d.   What are the future trends for theoretical orientations?

j.n.   There are at least two data-driven ways to address this question. The first method has been to systematically compare our recent findings on American clinical psychologists to those obtained in 1960, 1973 and 1981. The thirty years of trends demonstrate the steady advances made by behavioural and cognitive traditions. In the past five years alone, cognitive therapy has doubled in popularity among clinical psychologists. Family systems have risen from 0 per cent essentially to 5 per cent in the past ten years. Concomitantly there has been a decline in the endorsement of conventional psychoanalysis and humanistic approaches.

A second methodological avenue has been to study psychotherapy experts' predictions on the future popularity of theoretical orientations (see Norcross, Alford and DeMichele, in press; Prochaska and Norcross 1982). Composite forecasts have family systems, cognitive therapy and integration/eclecticism leading the pack into the next millennium. Psychobiological and behavioural orientations round out the top five. Again, classical psychoanalysis is expected to decline in popularity.

Both methods converge on what's hot and what's not for the next decade.

w.d.   It seems like everybody's predicting the demise of psychoanalytic therapy, but it hasn't laid down and died.

j.n.   Lloyd Silverman (1976), several years ago, wrote a classic article with a title that paraphrased Mark Twain: 'Psychoanalytic theory: the reports of my death are greatly exaggerated'. Classical psychoanalysis is clearly diminishing in influence and popularity and it has for many years. However, the short-term or time-limited psychodynamic approaches, particularly in the interpersonal direction, will continue to impact the field. And psychoanalytically informed appreciation of client dynamics will remain valuable, even if psychoanalytic therapy is not the treatment of choice for those clients.

w.d.   To what extent is this issue influenced by changes in American society, such as third-party reimbursement systems moving towards making clinicians more accountable for the services they render?

j.n.   The cost-containment measures exerted an enormous impact on the movement to time-limited, present-centred, goal-focused therapies. Not surprisingly cognitive, family systems and, to a lesser extent, the integration movement do not espouse long-term treatment objectives. So, there is a certain simpatico here, but it is not the entire story. The lack of empirical outcome research on psychoanalytic psychotherapy also led those of a scientific bent to look elsewhere to replace or, at least, complement a psychoanalytic persuasion.

w.d.   Do practising therapists really use their theoretical orientations?

j.n.   My research and clinical experience argue strongly against the propositions that clinical practice can be atheoretical or that orientations are uninfluential. A case in point is the erroneous stereotype that theoretical orientations are intellectually pleasing, but do not really matter when doing clinical work. I hear this claim at least once a week from students or from colleagues. When we ask clinical psychologists to indicate how frequently their chosen theoretical orientations influence their practice, nine-tenths of them report that they always or frequently use them.

Of course, that finding does not address the comparative issue of how much theory influences clinical practice compared to other determinants. Comparatively speaking, we listed eighteen variables that can potentially affect therapeutic practice (Norcross and Prochaska 1983). Of these variables, theoretical orientation obtained the highest mean. Other items, representing possible situational, personal, political and financial influences on practice, received lower average ratings. Thus, I believe it is fair to conclude that practising clinicians believe they are influenced by theory in therapy; that is to say, an organized theory does count when sitting down with a client.

w.d.   They may think they are influenced by their orientations, but are they really in practice?

j.n.   A host of studies have addressed the question. One question is whether psychotherapists of similar theoretical persuasions practise more similarly to each other than they do to colleagues of other theoretical orientations. The answer is a convincing yes. Another question is whether external observers and clients experience what therapists do in the same way that therapists believe they do in theoretical terms. The answer is clearly no. Clients cannot experience the jargon, the methods, the highfalutin concepts that therapists employ. We shall discuss this issue more thoroughly in the next interview devoted to personal therapy, but I'm reminded of my own therapy wherein my therapist stated he had used a particular technique. I responded: 'I thought you were being honest and straightforward'. The client's experience of therapist behaviour is frequently incongruent with the therapist's perception of what he or she may be offering.

w.d.   To what extent are therapists satisfied with their theoretical orientations?

j.n.   Reasonably satisfied. To take one example, in one of our studies we asked how satisfied clinicians were with their chosen theory. Over 80 per cent responded in the positive. We found very few clinicians reporting dissatisfaction with the conceptual and technical aspects of their theoretical orientation. In all fairness, those who were very dissatisfied would have probably already switched to another theoretical orientation.

That is not to say, however, that improvements and enhancements are not desirable. If you frame the satisfaction question in a different manner, nearly every psychotherapist will admit to lacunae and inadequacies in their theoretical orientations. I would draw the distinction between overt dissatisfaction with a theoretical orientation and a broader willingness to adapt one's therapeutic repertoire. They are related but not isomorphic.

w.d.   To what extent do clinicians switch their orientations over the course of their careers?

j.n.   They certainly do switch orientations. How the question is posed in a particular study influences the number and type of theoretical shifts. On the average, aggregating across studies, mature clinicians by middle-age have switched primary theoretical allegiance two or three times since completion of their graduate training. Most shifts parallel theoretical developments in the *Zeitgeist*, for instance, behavioural to cognitive-behavioural, or psychoanalytic to psychodynamic. Another popular shift is from a pure form or brand name therapy to an integrative approach as clinicians become more experienced.

w.d.   Why do they change?

j.n.   Speaking with dozens of psychotherapists about this issue, I come away with three distinct patterns. The first is that clinicians have been indoctrinated in a single theoretical orientation during graduate school which they did not like at the time or shortly thereafter did not embrace. A second cluster of people inform me that their personal predilections and values have evolved, occasionally dramatically, and their orientation changes correspondingly. One psychotherapist recently told me that the birth of his child and his personal therapy underscored the importance of the ultimate questions and meaning in life as well as the salience of the therapeutic relationship. He transformed from a cognitive-behavioural perspective toward a humanistic-existential one.

A third possibility is that clinical experiences lead one to a theoretical transition. The old theoretical orientation was not as applicable or efficient or relevant as another one would be. In my practice, for instance, I have been impressed with the efficacy of the cognitive-behavioural treatment of chronic pain and have come to rely on that perspective in the treatment of people suffering from that disorder. My interpersonal/existential persuasion can inform my work with chronic pain sufferers, but I find it neither as effective nor as cost-efficient.

w.D.   You mentioned certain orientation shifts, the main one being from a particular school of therapy to a more integrative one. Is there any evidence that psychotherapists move the other way, from integrative back to pure form therapy?

J.N.   That's an interesting question and one I have not personally researched. Surely there must be. The difficulty lies in the paucity of longitudinal studies and the dangers of retrospective designs. One would need to use identical methodology and instrumentation over time to track shifts in theoretical orientation.

It's an intriguing possibility that therapists could have been integrative and, for some reason, return to the security and direction of the mother theory. The few people I have known who did so initially adopted syncretism rather than genuine eclecticism, thereby becoming rather anxious, understandably so, in confronting the unstructured chaos of the therapeutic enterprise. They stated, in one form or another, 'It was easier when I knew exactly what to do at any given moment in psychotherapy'.

w.D.   In one of your articles, you distinguish between theoretical orientation as a binding religion and as a guiding formulation. Could you elaborate what you mean about this?

J.N.   Theoretical orientations are organized sets of concepts with which some clinicians find themselves agreeing, and do not constitute a rigorous set of rituals which one must worship. It's a voluntary decision to label oneself an adherent of a specific orientation, and that does not constitute a lifetime commitment of strict adherence. Good clinicians are flexible and good theories are widely applicable.

This is the critical distinction between theory-bound and theory-based practice. Few clinicians report being securely, exclusively bound to the doctrine of a single theory.

Along these lines, I also like to separate the actual theory from a few dogmatic proponents of that theory. Theory itself does not prohibit free exploration and sharing of contributions from other systems, but individuals. We occasionally throw the 'baby out with the bath water' by blaming theories of psychopathology and psychotherapy when, I believe, it is more appropriate to criticize the sterile attitudes of a few inveterate clinicians.

w.d.   Fine. We looked a little at the impact of theoretical orientations upon clinical practice. Is there any influence of orientation on the self-change mechanisms that therapists use in their own lives?

j.n.   There are literally hundreds of studies documenting the significant relationships between the therapists' theoretical orientation and their values, personalities, actual in-therapy behaviour, simulated in-therapy behaviour, rating behaviour, recall of therapy session, work practices, attitudes of therapy, and so on. At the levels of global theory and specific techniques, there are robust differences among theoretical orientations with the important exception of therapists' interpersonal skills. In this respect, my interest in the topic evolved to an intermediate level of analysis, between theory and technique, called the processes of change or the strategies of change. These are broadly defined as trans-theoretical means by which change occurs in psychotherapy. Examples are the opportunity for catharsis, providing feedback, practice of new behaviours.

Jim Prochaska and I became curious about the change processes that psychotherapists use in helping *clients* overcome distress, particularly in relation to change processes that they use in helping *themselves* overcome distress. For this, we developed two forms of the Processes of Change Scale. The first form, Therapist-Treat-Patient, consisted of items with the prefix 'I encourage my clients to', 'I point out to my clients that', or some similar therapy intervention. The second form, Therapist-Treat-Self, possessed the same item content and numerical order, except that the prefix was altered to 'I engage', 'I recall', or some similar self-intervention.

Regarding the impact of the clinician's theoretical orientations, the results of three studies (Norcross and Prochaska 1986a;

Norcross, Prochaska and Hambrecht, in press; Prochaska and Norcross 1983) indicated that therapists' clinical efforts with patients varied reliably as a function of orientation. Cognitive-behaviour therapists, to take one example, use significantly more counter-conditioning, contingency control and stimulus control than their psychoanalytic and psychodynamic colleagues. Psycho-dynamic therapists, by contrast, reported employing catharsis and the helping relationship significantly more frequently than their behavioural counterparts. Thus, all the observed differences were consistent with theoretical prescription.

This is not surprising; in fact, quite expected. The question that then arose was: Are psychotherapists equally influenced by theories in treating themselves?

No significant differences were found among psychotherapists' self-change due to orientation or experience. This pattern has been replicated in three separate studies, and I am unable to discern even a few statistical differences expected by chance alone. All of the composite findings strongly argue for a considerable degree of similarity among psychotherapists in their own self-change.

w.d. Why do you think that should be so? Why do you think therapists are influenced by their theories in helping their patients but not in helping themselves?

j.n. By replicating and expanding the original study – using different samples and clinical disorders – we were able to discard several initial hypotheses. For example, I thought the differential pattern might be attributable to age or gender or intelligence differences between therapists and their patients. These were shown not to be the operative factors.

I now offer two interpretations for the results. The first is a cynical perspective on the duplicity between psychotherapists' public careers and their personal lives. Psychotherapists may not avail themselves of what they offer their patients. Negatively stated, one may not necessarily have 'to practise what one preaches'. Or, as George Kelly might have said, we do not apply our theories reflexively. That is we do not apply the same theories to our own behaviour as psychologists that we use in understanding and treating others. In fact, in writing one of the early papers, I wanted to title it 'What's Good for the Goose is *Not* Good for the Gander!' Cooler heads prevailed and we ended up with a more conventional title, 'Psychotherapists' Perspectives on Treating Themselves and Their Clients for Psychic Distress'.

The second and more positive explanation is that psychotherapists become more pragmatic, eclectic and, if you will, secular
when they confront their own distress compared with confronting
clients' distress. This view is reminiscent of the contention that
experienced psychotherapists think quite similarly; a therapeutic
'underground', as Paul Wachtel (1977) has discussed. Consistent
with this explanation is evidence that the vast majority of behaviour
therapists choose *non*-behavioural personal treatment for themselves. On a personal, if not professional level, clinicians may be
taking the recent surge of eclecticism to heart.

W.D.   Surely if that were so, that would be manifested in the research
by the fact there should be quite a bit of variety in the self-change
process?

J.N.   There is. The overall variability as evidenced by standard
deviations does increase from psychotherapists treating clients to
treating themselves. It is important to recall that I'm not suggesting that the specific techniques a psychoanalyst may use in
understanding and treating his or her distress would not differ
from what a behaviourist might do under the same circumstances.
Rather we are focusing on mid-level processes, the basic strategies
they employ. These do not differ according to clinicians'
orientations when distress is on their front porch compared to
someone else's front porch.

W.D.   I see. Do you have any evidence that they may be using
different techniques to implement these strategies?

J.N.   No, we have no evidence for that, which is why we found it
essential to demonstrate that the strategies for treating patients still
differ according to theoretical orientation. The fact that psychotherapists employ differential strategies for clients, but not for
themselves, generates a more robust flavour of the results.
Otherwise one can attribute the findings to this mid-level of
abstraction rather than to a consensus of self-change among
psychotherapists.

W.D.   Do you have any future plans for research in this area?

J.N.   We have now replicated the original study three times, using
different populations, clinical disorders and other refinements,
particularly in describing the client in identical terms as the
therapist. We asked therapists to respond in terms of a client who
was of their intelligence and their professional background to rule
out the initial hypothesis that therapists may treat clients differentially because clients weren't as bright or as psychologically

advanced as therapists are. Having done that, I have no particular plans for investigating the matter further.

However, I do have further plans for exploring in detail and, perhaps longitudinally, psychotherapists' self-change. One of our original motivations for conducting these investigations was that doctoral-level psychotherapists are among the most educated and experienced behaviour change agents. And yet, at least publicly, we know embarrassingly little of what they offered themselves. Here we have this rich, untapped source of experts, and we don't know what they offer themselves that could be applied to laypersons.

The findings may not always be favourable to the helping professions. I dreaded the possibility that we might discover something parallel to a horribly obese, chain-smoking physician warning his or her patients to watch their weight and to cut their tobacco abuse. Fortunately we haven't discovered anything along these lines. None the less, we have discovered that a few psychotherapists are not particularly effective self-changers, and this contributes to their seeking personal therapy regularly.

w.d.   I wonder if we had an opportunity to look at the self-change processes of founders of specific theoretical orientations that we might not find a correlation between the processes they use with themselves and the processes they use with their clients. I'm thinking again of Albert Ellis and . . .

j.n.   That's interesting. I immediately was thinking of Sigmund Freud . . .

w.d.   We can explore that. Let's take Ellis first. Ellis has overcome certain problems on his own by methods which are now commonly used in rational-emotive therapy.

j.n.   And Freud immediately comes to my mind. His lengthy, enlightening self-analysis, particularly dream work, resulted in many of his dream fragments and condensed dreams being published in the landmark *Interpretation of Dreams*. Free associ-ation, examination of slips, and dream analysis became the corner-stones of early psychoanalysis.

w.d.   The effects might be much stronger for the founder of the school. The effects may weaken, so to speak, when second, third or fourth-generation therapists are the focus of the study.

j.n.   Linda Riebel (1982) has postulated a similar developmental pattern. She believes that therapists promulgate their theories by one of two mechanisms, either projecting their conflicts into their theories, such as Freud's Oedipal conflict, or by projecting their personality structures, such as Albert Ellis's conviction that irrationalities made him anxious. Psychotherapists with the greatest affinity for those psychological conflicts or personality structures gravitate toward that particular approach. But as this identification occurs over successive generations, as you point out, they don't have the power they once did.

It occurs to me a similar process has occurred in person-centred (client-centred) therapy. You mentioned earlier that it was on the decline, partially because the essence of client-centred therapy has been incorporated into the mainstream of contemporary psychotherapeutic approaches. Therapist expression of warmth, genuineness and empathy has literally been swallowed up, and one is then left with a vision of humankind. Carl Rogers's vision of humans, which he considered essential to his approach, has filtered out over the years.

w.d.   Let's look at your own relationship between your self-change processes and the processes you use with your clients.

j.n.   That's a dirty trick, Windy! As I reflect on it, I can honestly say that they are fairly similar. I try to practise what I preach, which is one of the explicit objectives of the transtheoretical approach – to integrate self-change and therapy change. In general, I emphasize the awareness–action connection: becoming cognitively and emotionally aware of why I'm distressed and then working to modify the cause or at least to reduce the distress.

For example, one of my convenient rationalizations is that I'm harried because I'm overworked. If that were the case, I believe both of us would be perpetually harried. I try to understand what I'm telling myself, what I'm feeling, what repetitive relationship patterns I'm enacting before I try to change myself. I would probably help clients reduce their distress more quickly through medication or through behavioural methods than I would do for myself.

As I reflect, I am aware of one discrepancy. You would probably have to strap me down to get me to take psychotropic medication, in part because I fear it and in part because, like many psychologists, I view medication as a mild failure. I'd have to be experiencing a far greater severity of distress than my patients before I would consider medication. I have at my disposal greater coping resources, psychological knowledge and better tolerance for discomfort than clients. On the other hand, I am probably more sensitive to physical pain than they – perhaps balancing this out. I might reach for a physical painkiller before clients would.

w.d.   One piece of folklore is that clinicians become interested in a theoretical orientation because it seems to be consistent with the ways they've been helping themselves. Is this piece of folklore a myth?

j.n.   No, I think there is considerable validity to that position. In one of our studies (Norcross and Prochaska 1983), we asked psychotherapists why they were drawn to their theoretical orientations. Topping the list was a personal fit with their own personality and a convergence of the theory's concepts and methods with their own life.

It leads me to speculate why a clinician might be drawn toward eclecticism. Speaking personally and off the top of my head, I would say that I find both awareness and action strategies useful. There are few psychotherapy systems besides eclecticism that equally weight awareness/insight processes and action processes as well as balance relationship stances and technical interventions. In my own life, personal treatment and self-change should be equally weighted as well.

w.d.   An interesting picture is emerging. Clinicians become interested in theoretical orientations because there is a match between their own self-change processes and that of their theoretical orientation. Their orientation then influences the change processes that they use with their clients. But somewhere along the line the relationship between their own change processes and the theoretical orientation alters in some way. What do think is going on?

j.n.   Part of what may be going on is that experienced clinicians realize that no one theory has a monopoly on truth or utility. They continue to experiment within their theoretical orientations and between theoretical orientations, particularly in their own self-change. In discussing these phenomena with colleagues, they gravitate to approaches that best complement the weakness of their particular orientation.

Take one recent example: a prominent psychoanalyst was having health-related problems and suddenly learned progressive muscle relaxation and autogenic training. However, he did so only for himself, never with his patients. He believed that the autogenic training was probably outside of his clinical expertise, but did begin to refer his own analytic patients to a colleague for autogenic training.

w.d.   An interesting relationship – we perhaps become eclectic or integrative with ourselves before doing so with our patients.

j.n.   Yes, the paradigm shift starts at home, so to speak. In this sense, psychotherapy integration is well underway.

5 | PERSONAL THERAPY

WINDY DRYDEN   John, in this interview I want to explore another one of your interests and that is personal therapy. First of all, in your view, how important is personal therapy as a prerequisite for clinical practice?

JOHN NORCROSS   I consider personal therapy a highly desirable, if not necessary, experience for clinical practitioners. Perhaps, Freud (1937/1964) put it best in *Analysis Terminable and Interminable*: 'where and how is the poor wretch to acquire the ideal qualifications which he will need in this profession? The answer is in an analysis of himself, with which his preparation for his future activity begins.'

The importance of personal therapy as a prerequisite varies directly as a function of a number of variables. One is the degree of characterological pathology of the prospective therapist; a second variable is the emotional and interpersonal intensity of the psychotherapy the prospective therapist plans to offer. Reasonably healthy clinicians offering behaviour therapy exclusively, for instance, might require therapy less than a colleague conducting psychodynamic therapy.

None the less, my research and experience lead me to strongly recommend personal therapy for all my trainees, but I stop short of requiring it, which feels authoritarian to me. But I push it and continually remind them that, second only to practical experience, personal psychotherapy is rated by practising clinicians as the most important contributor to their professional development.

W.D.   How did you first get interested in this area?

J.N.   My interest predated my own personal therapy, but the therapy experience intensified the interest. Initially it struck me as a logical and important area to research. What troubles a troubleshooter?

What do we learn from our own treatment? How do care-givers give themselves care? There is so much yet to be learned about the practice of psychotherapy, about the person of the therapist and, of course, about ourselves by examining personal treatment. I made a conscious effort not to contaminate my own treatment, an important personal experience, by conducting research or reading literature on the topic while I was in therapy.

w.d.   The research indicates that the relationship between clinicians who have had personal therapy and the outcome of their patients is not a strong one.

j.n.   That's correct. The literature is sparse and inconclusive. Under such circumstances one can conclude that the therapist's personal therapy is 'a matter of faith', as Wampler and Strupp (1976) once put it. Or one could also ask, what other lessons might be generated? If one considers the difficulty in evaluating psychotherapy outcome and the huge number of therapist variables which impact on outcome, we would not expect a strong and consistent relationship between the two. Instead, I expect a fairly subtle relationship, which crude measurement devices would be unable to discern. In this context, I don't find the lack of strong correspondence between the incidence of personal therapy and improved clinical outcome surprising or disappointing.

There are some convincing trends from therapists' reports on the lasting lessons they gained from personal therapy. Although these lessons may not directly transfer or generalize to clinical work, they probably have some effect. In a recent study (Norcross, Strausser and Missar 1988), we asked therapists to describe briefly the lasting lessons from their treatment experience. The four most common lessons all concerned interpersonal relationships and dynamics in psychotherapy: the importance of empathy and the personal relationship; the validity of transference and counter-transference; the need for patience and tolerance; and the use of the therapist's self. This heightened sensitivity to the therapeutic relationship may well translate into clinical practice, though again because of the measurement difficulties, not into consistently discernible outcome differences.

The incidence of personal therapy has been positively associated with the clinician's ability to display empathy, warmth and genuineness in at least two studies. Further, we have found increased emphasis on the therapeutic relationship among therapists who have had personal therapy in several empirical investigations. This pattern holds true for general samples of psychotherapists as well as psychoanalytic and behaviour therapists (see Norcross 1990b). It is particularly gratifying when our clinical truths match the empirical results.

w.d.   Let me clear up one point. Even the fact that the relationship between personal therapy and outcome isn't very strong . . .

j.n.   I don't accept your premise. I believe the relationship probably exists and is probably strong but we will never discern it given our conventional research designs. But I certainly agree that if one turns to the empirical literature you would have to use other criteria.

w.d.   Right. Would you then say that perhaps you're putting the case rather too strongly in recommending trainees to have personal therapy, certainly more strongly than the evidence warrants?

j.n.   I'm putting my recommendation for personal therapy more strongly than the available empirical evidence warrants; however, I think there are complementary sources of robust evidence which need to be considered. The consistently high ratings given to personal treatment by therapists who have completed it, the various rationales for why therapy might enhance the person of the therapist and the craft he or she practises.

A student once canvassed the literature for reasons to recommend personal therapy. We found six basic reasons and I believe there is sufficient clinical consensus and process literature to recommend personal therapy. For instance personal treatment improves the emotional functioning of the psychotherapist, thus making a clinician's life less neurotic and more gratifying. Personal therapy also offers intensive opportunities to observe clinical methods, thus modelling interpersonal and technical skills. Personal therapy places the therapist in the client role, which increases sensitivity to client reactions and respect for patients' struggles.

In sum, it is simply not a linear relationship that your therapy will dramatically improve your clinical outcome. The relationship is broader, more subtle than that; I'm resisting the impulse to state that the conclusions about personal therapy demonstrate the limitations of hard, empirical science, but essentially that's what I'm saying.

w.d.   What proportion of psychotherapists elect to receive psychotherapy?

j.n.   The prevalence of personal treatment is stable over the years, at least in the United States. The best averages are: 75–76 per cent of psychologists, 67 per cent of psychiatrists, and 65–72 per cent of clinical social workers. By comparison, the lifetime incidence of *any* type of mental health treatment for laypersons is between 10 per cent and 25 per cent of the population.

w.d.   To what extent have psychotherapists gone back to personal therapy after being trained?

j.n.   As is so often the case, Freud (1937/1964) anticipated your question many years ago. He recommended that the clinician reinitiate personal treatment on the recognition that intense therapy continually exposes the clinician to the impact of the patients' unconscious processes. He exhorted every therapist to periodically, at intervals of five years or so, submit himself to analysis once more, without feeling ashamed of taking that step.

Following Freud's exhortations, practising psychotherapists do in fact utilize the very services they provide. In three recent studies (see Norcross 1990b), over one-half of responding clinicians received personal therapy following completion of formal training. It is an illusion, or perhaps a delusion, that most mental health professionals do not experience a need for personal therapy once they are in practice.

w.d.   Is it true that behaviour therapists seek personal therapy less frequently than therapists of other persuasions?

j.n.   Yes. Somewhere between 47 per cent and 59 per cent of self-identified behaviour therapists have sought personal therapy during their lives. This percentage and the average duration of the personal therapy are significantly lower than their colleagues of other persuasions. For instance, 85–95 per cent of psychoanalysts and 75–80 per cent of eclectics seek therapy.

w.d.   Why do you think this is so?

j.n.   The reason for this disparity is a matter of speculation, of course. Most observers agree that behaviour therapy does not emphasize personal therapy's importance, say, compared to psychoanalysts, in training. Most observers also agree that the role definition of behaviour therapists – modifying behaviour in the capacity of an educator – reduces the emotional and intra-psychic involvement for which personal therapy might be particularly indicated. I have also heard mean-spirited perspectives on the disparity, mainly that behaviour therapists are repressed in their personalities and in their treatment orientation and therefore they are less disposed to seek therapy involvement for themselves.

w.d.   What are typical presenting problems that psychotherapists bring when they seek out therapy?

j.n.   One of our first hypotheses was that therapists' personal treatment was primarily a component of formal graduate or post-graduate training. But this was rarely the case. When we asked over 500 psychologists, psychiatrists and social workers why they entered therapy – for personal reasons, for professional purposes, or both – the majority indicated that they entered primarily for personal reasons. Only 10 per cent replied that their treatment was largely for training reasons, and the remaining one-third entered for both personal and professional growth.

What then troubles the troubleshooters? The three most frequent presenting issues for therapists were marital conflicts, depression and anxiety. Other common problems are interpersonal difficulties, family-of-origin concerns, need for self-understanding and career decisions. These chief concerns are quite similar to those presented by the general population.

w.d.   How does that fit in with what we were talking about in our prior interview concerning the stresses and strains that therapists encounter in what has been called an 'impossible profession?'

j.n.   The increased incidence of personal therapy for therapists is probably related to the stresses and strains that we encounter in our work. Psychotherapists' most frequent reasons for seeking therapy coincide perfectly with the research indicating that clinical practice exacts a negative toll on the practitioner, particularly in the form of problematic anxiety, moderate depression and emotional underinvolvement with family members.

Another part of the story, seemingly obvious but frequently neglected, is that psychotherapists are people too. Their lives are full of problems, like everyone else, and these problems run the entire gamut of human concerns. In our last study (Norcross and Prochaska 1986a), therapists reported encountering ordinary life problems: infidelity, alcoholism, divorce, murder of an old friend, a child's suicide, drug use, a brother on trial for murder, just to name a few. But the point is that to ameliorate the distinctive problems of living, one has also to be human and that means to have problems like everyone else. Therapists receive a 'double whammy' – life problems like everyone else plus the strains of an 'impossible profession'.

w.d.   And when they choose their own therapists, how do they go about this? What criteria do they value in selecting their own personal therapists?

J.N.   We recently conducted a study on this very issue (Norcross, Strausser and Faltus 1988). Over 500 psychotherapists rated the influence of a multitude of variables on the selection of their psychotherapists. The consensual top five selection criteria were the therapist's competence, clinical experience, his or her professional reputation, warmth and caring, and openness. That is therapists chose their own therapists primarily on the basis of clinical acumen and interpersonal qualities.

What we learned that may be useful in conducting psychotherapy is that these therapist-patients seek a personal relationship with therapists, one in which they feel affirmed and appreciated by another human whom they like and respect (see Grunebaum 1983). That this holds true for a very psychologically sophisticated group, as well as for more naive patients, corroborates the view that these factors are the *sine qua non* of effective psychological treatment. Relatedly, the most frequent reason advanced for harmful treatment experiences among psychotherapists in one of our studies (Norcross, Strausser and Missar 1988) and in one by Henry Grunebaum (1986) is a rigid, distant and uninvolved therapeutic relationship.

W.D.   Didn't Grunebaum also find that a harmful experience was receiving personal treatment from a therapist who became overinvolved with him?

J.N.   Yes, and I certainly believe that occurs. But in his particular study, there was a confound in that he was soliciting responses from psychotherapists in the metropolitan Boston area. One of their primary selection criteria was to obtain a therapist outside of their own professional and social network because therapists were becoming overly involved in their lives, both personally and professionally. This apparently occurs less in other areas of the country than it does in Boston. None the less, his study speaks to the need for a golden mean or the Aristotelian median, the proper level of therapeutic involvement.

W.D.   Which criteria did you find concerning therapist selection that proved not to be important?

J.N.   One selection criterion deemed unimportant was the research productivity of the prospective therapist. This was rated as an unimportant, almost negligible, factor in selection decisions. This finding reminded me that academic standing and clinical expertise are probably independent dimensions. Perhaps I needed to be reminded of that because I'm an academic.

A second relatively unimportant role was the cost per session. I was rather surprised that this was not rated higher since clients are concerned with fees, and this finding may reflect the higher income status of psychotherapists' occupation. But in 'shrink choice', as in life itself, you typically receive what you pay for.

w.d.   What about issues like theoretical orientation of one's personal therapist, gender, and to what profession they belong. Are they important?

j.n.   We closely examined the characteristics of chosen therapists in terms of gender, profession, and theoretical orientation. In terms of gender, male therapists were chosen by 82 per cent of our male respondents and by 67 per cent of our female respondents; 33 per cent of the women and 18 per cent of the men received personal treatment from a female. However, the statistical analyses determined that an increasing proportion of women therapists are now seeking women as a therapist.

In terms of professional discipline, psychotherapists seek treatment from psychiatrists, psychologists, social workers, counsellors and lay analysts in that general order. There are definite preferences on the basis of professional discipline, however. Psychologists received treatment from fellow psychologists most often, followed by psychiatrists. Psychiatrists routinely sought out other psychiatrists about 80 per cent of the time.

w.d.   Was any reason given for that?

j.n.   No specific reason, although one possibility was that many of the psychiatrists were in classic psychoanalytic training. At that time, since psychiatrists had a monopoly on analytic institutes, personal therapy with a psychiatrist was virtually mandated. Social workers, interestingly, were the only professional group more likely to enter treatment with a therapist of a discipline different from their own. If they had their preference, they would see a psychologist. Younger psychotherapists are increasingly seeking assistance from psychologists as well.

In several respects, the trend of mental health professionals being treated by members of their own gender and discipline are quite heartening. It can enhance personal validation and professional socialization. In other respects, however, this emerging pattern can promote professional indoctrination and theoretical 'inbreeding'.

w.d.   Now, let's take a closer look at theoretical orientation. Do therapists seek out personal therapists of similar or different theoretical orientations?

J.N.   They seek out therapists who are, as a rule, similar to their own theoretical orientation. Let me give you a few examples: in nearly all the cases, 90 per cent or so, psychoanalytic respondents received psychoanalytic or psychodynamic treatment. Behaviourists were the least restrictive in their choice: 44 per cent chose an eclectic, 19 per cent a cognitivist, 19 per cent a humanist, 12 per cent a psychoanalyst, and only 6 per cent a fellow behaviourist in our most recent study.

W.D.   That parallels with what Arnold Lazarus (1971) found about twenty years ago.

J.N.   Yes. Our results, paralleling his reports, indicated that fewer than one in ten behaviourists choose behavioural treatment for themselves. Rather, they prefer eclectic, psychoanalytic and humanistic therapists by a margin of more than two to one over behavioural treatment. It is also of interest that relatively few non-behavioural psychotherapists, only about 5 per cent across studies, elected behaviour therapy for themselves.

W.D.   How do we account for that?

J.N.   Wolpe (1981; 1988) and I (1989a; Wogan and Norcross 1982) have tangled twice in print on the meaning of these findings. Wolpe argued that these data bespeak unmatched cynicism and hypocrisy on the part of behaviour therapists, if the data are valid. His explanation is that our research method permitted clinicians to self-identify their theoretical orientations, and the behaviour therapists are not 'genuine' behaviour therapists in his eyes. This may be the case, but we used self-identification for all theoretical orientations.

Two alternative attributions seem more likely to me. First, few behaviour therapists – self-identified or Wolpe-approved – were available when clinicians sought personal treatment many years ago. Second, increased awareness and personal growth are highly valued goals for a therapist's own therapy. Symptom alleviation *per se* was rated the least important of all outcome measures in one study (Buckley, Karasu and Charles 1981) of psychotherapists' personal treatment, although I readily comprehend that it may not be so for Wolpe. As Arnie Lazarus (1971) articulated in the 1970s, if one does not have a specific disabling disorder, behaviour therapy would not be the treatment of choice. He was quick to say that this did not speak to any duplicity on the part of behaviour therapists, but different therapies have different goals.

w.d.   We have now looked at the relationship between having personal therapy and clinical outcome with one's own patients. Looking more broadly, to what extent are therapists generally satisfied with the results of their own personal therapy? How effective is it in their own lives?

j.n.   Cutting to the chase, aren't we? The most reliable data are the self-reported outcomes of therapist-patients themselves. These are consistently positive: over 90 per cent of the therapist-patients indicate improvement in terms of behaviour/symptomatology, cognitions/insight and emotions/relief. On each change dimension, only 2 per cent or 3 per cent reported any deterioration. So the research to date reveals that the majority receive considerable personal and professional benefit from personal treatment. Satisfactory outcomes are probably achieved more regularly than is suggested by the impression prevalent in the literature or in private conversations.

w.d.   Are there any negative effects?

j.n.   As in all psychotherapy, a minority of therapists do report negative outcome and actual harm as a result of treatment. Henry Grunebaum (1983; 1986) has investigated this in a series of studies. In our sample (Norcross, Strausser and Missar 1988), 8 per cent answered positively to the question, 'Was your therapy or analysis harmful in any way?' We then tried to identify covariates of these harmful therapy experiences by examining characteristics of the therapists conducting the therapy.

   We discovered three substantial differences: therapists who were younger, who were counsellors, and who were behaviourally or eclectically oriented were more likely to conduct treatment that the therapist-patient perceived as harmful. Should these patterns be replicated, the referral advice is to avoid young, behaviourally or eclectically oriented counsellors. My suspicion is that their relative inexperience and neglect of the therapeutic alliance might be the culprits.

w.d.   Now, I believe that *Psychology Today* in July 1989 identified you as 'the therapist's therapist'. What did they mean by that?

j.n.   I believe they meant that a higher proportion of my caseload was comprised of fellow therapists and that I have a reputation for conducting research on the topic. At any one time, approximately one-third of my clients are mental health professionals. This may be a little higher than average, but most psychotherapists in my experience routinely see other therapists for treatment.

w.d.   Why do you think you have such a reputation?

j.n.   Probably a number of reasons. One is that I conduct considerable research on personal therapy in particular and on the person of
the therapist in general. Another would be an academic affiliation,
which tends to generate recognition.

One under-recognized reason is my integrative treatment
orientation. I have no need to indoctrinate peers into a single
'school' and I have no theoretical axe to grind.

Another reason, a little embarrassing to mention, is that I am a
good therapist. At least, I am committed and straightforward,
which when it comes to working with other therapists, is not as
common as one would hope.

w.d.   Why are you embarrassed to say that?

j.n.   It sounds immodest and self-promoting. I have similar difficulties with advertising and marketing clinical services, although I
recognize its necessity in this era. I do not envision myself as a
healer with large telephone directory advertisements or distributing business cards.

w.d.   So we can say that you're a healer, but not a spieler.

j.n.   Very punny!

w.d.   Let's look more closely at your experience of working with
other therapists as clients. Are there particular differences that you
have identified in attempting to help a therapist versus other
patients who are not part of the profession?

j.n.   There is a veiled secrecy, a taboo, against open examination of
the psychotherapist's own treatment. Mutually protective dynamics operate with which therapists and patients implicitly
collude to ignore. That's where the differences emerge: difficulty
in acknowledging personal limitations. Clinicians can suffer from
the occupational hazard of grandiosity and, accordingly, struggle
to accept patienthood, a sense of being one-down after what they
regard as being one-up for so much of the day.

Another reason for my reputation as a therapist's therapist, come
to think of it, may be my emphasis on a collaborative therapeutic
relationship. I do not regard the participants as being either one-up
or one-down. I endorse a more mutual relationship.

Another persistent disparity I experience is an over-intellectual,
pseudo-insightful, sophisticated defence among psychotherapists.
A pervasive tendency to talk about, rather than to work on,
conflicts. Since psychotherapists are comparatively less interested

in symptom relief and specific behaviour change, there can be lots of talk, not all particularly productive.

Another distinctive danger that comes to mind is also simultaneously a pleasure, namely the therapist's ego gratification in treating other therapists. The danger lies in an inflated notion of our own skill, when modesty should prevail. I experience ego gratification in being recognized and published as 'the therapist's therapist' and yet, if I begin to believe it, it might represent the beginning of the end of being a decent therapist with other therapists.

W.D.   What other satisfactions are there in treating other therapists?

J.N.   The typical satisfactions in treating any client, but also some distinctive elements. Therapists are typically bright, verbal, psychologically minded, and therefore receptive to exploration of their interior life. That makes it joyful at times, presuming you get through the intellectual shit first, putting it bluntly.

I also recognize a probable impact, a ripple-effect, that successful treatment with therapists will have on their patients and their patient's interpersonal world. In a sense, as in providing consultation and indirect service, personal therapy with therapists helps more clients than I could ever personally treat. And arising out of my particular interest in the person of the therapist, conducting therapy with therapists provides a unique opportunity to learn more about the person of the therapist. Motivations for selecting the profession, stressors and satisfactions, the private, real-life experience of becoming and being a psychotherapist – peeking behind the professional mask.

W.D.   Let me end this by discussing my own experiences of personal therapy which may have a bearing on this issue. I have mentioned elsewhere (Dryden and Branco Vasco 1991) that my own experiences of personal therapy were not that productive; partly because I found it difficult to share the therapists' theoretical ideas. Their attempts to make sense of what I was saying led to conflicts between my world-view and theirs. On the other hand, I would not seek out a cognitive-behaviour therapist because I strongly suspect that I might spend half my time supervising him or her.

J.N.   Interesting predicament. If you go for more of the same, you could end up critiquing the therapist and perhaps not learning much. If you go for something different, you confront a paradigm clash and part of you resists the differences.

w.d.   Right. I resolve the differences by annually talking with Albert Ellis, who thinks like me.

j.n.   Arthur Burton (1972) many years ago recommended something along those lines. An annual satisfaction check-up for an hour or so with a master therapist, to check the frustrations and to see how one's getting on. You certainly have sought out the services of a master therapist, the founder of RET.

w.d.   During the therapy session we talk about other things and I might even bring in the issues. And this raises another question. Does personal therapy with therapists as clients overlap with supervision of their clinical work?

j.n.   There is certainly a component of clinical supervision that approaches personal therapy. Counter-transference, interpersonal elicitations, clinician's life difficulties permeate the therapeutic hour and thus are appropriate grist for supervision. However, it is my standard practice to separate the two and not to allow therapists, especially trainees, to transform their therapy hour into a supervision hour or vice versa. That can be a defence, but it's also quite understandable in another sense.

w.d.   Are there any differences between working with therapists as clients when the therapists are starting out in their profession as opposed to when they are more experienced?

j.n.   Yes and no. Taking the no, I would fall back on Henry Stack Sullivan's one genus postulate: people are fundamentally more alike than different. I see therapists as therapists and human no matter what their career stage.

Taking the yes, the typical transference relationship and the recurrent conflict material they bring in tend to be different. Trainees are at a different place in terms of finances, authority conflicts, and the relationships they create with me. I am viewed, rightly or wrongly, as a member of the training establishment. Should they be having difficulties responding to a particular supervisor or programme director, they frequently manifest that conflict in our therapeutic relationship even though I am independent of their training programme. The conflicts neophyte therapists raise are typically more urgent, financially oriented and reality-grounded, and for that reason I enjoy working with them. Established mental health professionals, unless they are impaired, are generally earning more and in a comfortable life niche. So I'm particularly fond of seeing students on a reduced fee scale for that reason, as my schedule permits.

6

CLINICAL TRAINING

WINDY DRYDEN In this interview, John, I'd like to look at your views on clinical training. In light of your intensive involvement in this area, how do you think we should select the best therapists?

JOHN NORCROSS Very carefully and in concert with the empirical research on effective psychotherapists. First and foremost, I would choose those students with facilitative interpersonal skills – warm, empathic, caring, respectful, committed. The literature, from my reading, is compelling on this point – the single best *therapist* variable that predicts positive outcome is interpersonal skills. Unfortunately the selection process is frequently reversed in that interpersonal skills are considered secondary to academic performance, which bears little relation to therapeutic competence.

From that point, I would adhere to three criteria advanced by Holt and Luborsky in the 1950s. Their studies (1958) compiled experts' opinions on the personal qualities sought in applicants for psychotherapy training. The first therapist quality was an introspective orientation, the capacity to observe inner life, commit to self-observation, and engage in appropriate self-disclosure. The second valued quality was an intellectual predisposition – rational thought, dispassionate examination, disciplined action. The third is a relativistic perspective – the ability to accept individual differences, and to appreciate disparate contexts and values.

It should be clarified, of course, that these selection criteria apply to psychotherapists. My suggestions for selecting the best clinical psychologists or psychiatrists would extend these criteria. Statistical and research acumen for clinical psychologists, obviously a biomedical background for psychiatrists.

W.D. You have been openly critical of the way psychotherapy training is normally approached. Can you say what your difficulties are about this?

J.N.   We could spend at least an hour on this question alone, but I'll try to hit the 'low lights' of clinical training. Throughout my career I have been singularly impressed by our immense responsibilities and collective failures in training competent practitioners. Psychotherapy training in an academic environment is often just that – academic – long on exposition and short on experience (see Robertson 1984). This erosion of excellence, as Hans Strupp (1975) once called it, can be attributed to distorted institutional contingencies and confused personal priorities, but these do not excuse the training system, nor us personally, from dereliction of duty.

Where to start on specifics? I'll touch on a few. One is inadequate experience. Experience in applied settings is often optional, at least prior to internship. The principal complaint of psychotherapists surveyed following graduation is inadequate clinical experience and inconsistent clinical supervision.

Another critique is that we offer exposure rather than competence in training. According to Larry Beutler (Beutler *et al.* 1987), it is as though psychotherapy training programmes believe in the 'germ theory' of education. If you're exposed to the theory and the procedures you will catch them, thereafter being and remaining skilled. Training therapists to achieve a stated criterion of competence has seldom been attempted. Rather we rely on a host of criteria, most academic or temporal, that bear negligible relationships to clinical skills.

A further difficulty is that trainees are traditionally taught either in the isolated single theory approach or the multiple competing theory approach. The single theory concentration suggests that this is the one and only truth, while the multi-theory comparison suggests that no truth exists. The result is typically the production of either narrow adherents to rigid orthodoxy or a cohort of broadly based practitioners who possess a confused hodgepodge of half facts.

And a final criticism is that the training process is disjointed. The acquisition of psychotherapy skills tends to be a poorly co-ordinated process in most programmes. It is not unusual to encounter students whose entire clinical experience rests on one theory or one modality. Few training programmes offer an articulated and systematic curriculum designed to ensure competence in multiple theories and formats.

w.d.   One viewpoint in Britain concerning the development of counsellors is that it's better to train them in a specific approach first and then to broaden out later, rather than to start by trying to develop integrative or eclectic therapists. What's your viewpoint on this issue?

J.N.   Somewhere in the confused middle. If students were truly trained to competence, rather than assumed competence by their faculty, in one theoretical approach *and* if students were willing to differentially refer outside their theoretical predilection when appropriate, then I would have no difficulties whatsoever with the 'one approach' training strategy. You are quite correct that learning several approaches simultaneously or within a few years to competence is a most arduous and ambitious task. However, without competence in several psychotherapy systems or the guarantee of differential referral, clients are at constant risk of mistreatment. As a consequence, I take a middle position in stating that our current training system is inadequate and in recommending an overhaul of the system toward what I call an ideal training system.

w.d.   And what would that ideal system look like?

J.N.   I will provide an outline of this idealistic integrative training, knowing full well that it's skimpy and probably beyond the existing resources of most programmes. But let me offer a parallel: imagine a student graduating from medical or dental school and the graduate not possessing the capacity to perform competently, nor particularly willing or eager to refer. I doubt we would let many of those institutions remain open though we tend to cast a blind eye toward inadequate psychotherapy training.

In any event, the ideal psychotherapy education would encompass an interlocking sequence of training experiences predicated on the crucial therapist-mediated and therapist-provided determinants of psychotherapy outcome. This sequence is written up in more detail with Larry Beutler and John Clarkin (Norcross, Beutler and Clarkin, 1990) in *Systematic Treatment Selection*. The suggested training programme consists of five steps; as you will see, the integration comes toward the end.

The first step is training in fundamental relationship and communication skills, such as active listening, non-verbal communication, empathy, modelling, and regard for patient problems. Acquisition of these generic interpersonal skills would follow one of the systematic modules that have empirically demonstrated significant training effects compared to less specified programmes. Students would be retained in this foundation course until a predefined level of competence was achieved, not simply because they completed the course with a grade of *B* or because the Fall term had ended.

The second interlocking step is an exploration of various models of human behaviour. The course would explore in some depth psychoanalytic, humanistic-existential, cognitive-behavioural, interpersonal-systems, and social-anthropological theories of human functioning and dysfunction. At this point, students would be exposed to all approaches without judgement being made as to their relative contributions to 'truth'.

w.d.   And the third step?

j.n.   The third step is a course on theories of psychotherapy. At the outset, multiple systems of psychotherapy would be presented critically but within a paradigm of comparison and integration. Students would be encouraged to adopt tentatively that perspective which is most harmonious with their own values and which engenders their own preferences.

The fourth step in this sequence is a series of practica. Neophyte therapists would be expected to become competent, that is to demonstrate competence, in the use of at least two systems of psychotherapy that vary in therapeutic objectives. In both cases, completion of the practicum would depend on specific criteria to ensure acquisition of the skills associated with a given approach. Relevant psychotherapy handbooks and treatment manuals would be used to outline the criteria.

Following completion of these competency-based courses, the fifth and final step is the integration of disparate models and methods. The emerging consensus in the United States and apparently in Britain is that the sophisticated adoption of an integrative perspective occurs after various therapy systems and techniques have been learned. This formal course on psychotherapy integration would provide a decisional model for selecting the procedures from various therapeutic orientations to be applied in given circumstances and with given clients.

w.d.   That's interesting. A different way of perhaps approaching the same end would be to take an integrative system, like Egan's (1975), which is an integrative process model and which shows that you need different skills at different times in the therapeutic process. Consequently the training is concerned with helping trainees to develop competencies, as you put it, in the skills at each point in the model.

J.N.   What would you do with clients who require skills beyond the student's competence?

W.D.   The ideal would be for students to demonstrate proficiency at the various skills before they see clients. Then they are supervised according to client needs.

J.N.   That's a similar claim made in training institutes: 'We'll train our students to be competent in psychoanalysis or behaviourism, for example, and we will be careful to select only those clients who are most appropriate for our students.' However, this is rarely done in my experience, and to be blunt, I think the claim is a fraud.

W.D.   It's a fraud because . . .?

J.N.   Because training and clinic directors make unsubstantiated claims about the selection of clients for that particular student. I have been personally involved in several training clinics and have visited dozens that profess to carefully match client needs and trainee competencies. Without exception, when I speak with students and enquire about their experience, they tell me that clients are not carefully screened and comprehensively evaluated to match students. If it would occur, then it would be a wonderful training system and we probably would have no need for a training sequence as ambitious as mine.

The training reality is that everyone seeks the so-called 'garden-variety neurotic', which translates into least seriously disturbed patients. There is little sophisticated differential referral occurring in training clinics. I realize that sounds scathing, but I do not see evidence to the contrary beyond well-meaning generalizations.

W.D.   In your opinion, when should trainees preferably see patients or clients in the training process?

J.N.   After they have demonstrated competence through simulations and role-plays with fellow students of the foundation interpersonal skills. I believe Egan's model overlaps largely with our first training step of foundation interpersonal skills. When students have demonstrated competence to their supervisor's satisfaction and to standardized criteria, then I would let them work with carefully screened patients who are not severely disturbed. College counselling centres, not coincidentally, are a popular setting for that early training, since the clientele is not that disturbed.

We also mistakenly assume that our more experienced clinical students, such as those with masters degrees, possess those foundation interpersonal skills. I believe we delude ourselves in such assumptions.

w.d.   Let's take the training stages you outlined one by one. Let's start with the foundation level skills. How would you advocate these being taught in class?

j.n.   The first day of the course, my objective is to convince students that the primacy of these skills for psychotherapy outcome is substantiated by robust research findings. Given the empirical side of me, I would use one of the training modules, which have been shown to out-perform less specified programmes, to teach (or review) such skills as active listening, empathic responses and so forth. There are a number of excellent programmes for this purpose, including human relations training and Ivey's (Ivey and Authier 1978) micro-counselling approach. I would use their text and the accompanying workbook, and would have students make many tapes, including a systematic pre-training to post-training comparison of their work. Students would be retained in this course of practicum and not be assigned to training cases until they met a predefined level of competence.

w.d.   Let's take the second and third levels now, John, which involve presenting various models of human behaviour and psychotherapy.

j.n.   How would I go about that? For that second step of exploring various models of human behaviour, I would focus on six or seven major models by assigning readings of the primary literature in those areas. In the case of psychoanalysis, I would have them read Freud in the original, not some homogenized textbook coverage. Margaret Mead's writings could form the bases of social-anthropological topics. So for an entire semester, we would consider diverse ways of conceptualizing how people function with an emphasis on cross-cultural functioning. The next semester would be a variant of the popular theories of counselling or systems of psychotherapy course. In this course, which I actually teach, I employ Jim Prochaska's (1984) *Systems of Psychotherapy* textbook which summarizes and compares the various systems of psychotherapy and offers a cogent critique of each system's advantages and limitations. His integrative model emphasizes the complementarity of the various models. I also assign an adjunct text for additional case material, either Wedding and Corsini's (1989) *Case Studies in Psychotherapy* or Nolan Saltzman and my (1990) *Therapy Wars*. This engenders an informed pluralism, an intellectual relativity which potentially frames integration.

w.d.   Would that third step be just theoretical or would it have practical applications as well?

j.n.   At that point, it's entirely theoretical. We then move on to the fourth step, consisting of a series of practica. In this ideal training programme, we would offer five or six practica and students would select the two most harmonious with their own values. Integration builds on strengths and emphasizes complementarity; it does not destroy knowledge or detract from preferences. In this practicum step, students would demonstrate competence in at least two psychotherapy systems with varying therapeutic objectives. Unfortunately many students begin at the fourth step, assuming they have already met the preceding steps.

There is little credence in my view to clinical training 'by baptism' – by throwing students in the deep end with clients and having them survive or drown. A more educational and refined perspective would be to introduce clients gradually, as we do in practically every other important human endeavour. One does not throw fourth-grade students into calculus. One does not send first-year medical students to complete an appendectomy to see if they survive or drown. Psychotherapy training and mental health care deserve at least, if not more, attention to gradual and systematic training as other professions.

w.d.   What's the fifth step?

j.n.   The fifth step, following completion of the competency-based practica, is the integration of disparate models and methods. This is a formal psychotherapy integration and treatment selection course. For this seminar, which I have co-taught, I adopt Frances, Clarkin and Perry's (1984) *Differential Therapeutics in Psychiatry* and more recently, Beutler and Clarkin's (1990) *Systematic Treatment Selection*. It's the big picture of clinical practice. Where does everything come together? How does a psychotherapist recognize his or her strengths, as well as limitations, leading to prescriptive practice and differential referral?

w.d.   The picture I have is that, rather than providing an integration right at the start and helping people to develop an idea how the jigsaw fits together, your model begins with the foundation skills and leads towards integration.

j.n.   Yes, and that progression is based on our knowledge of how people learn. One example would be Perry's (1970) work on the development of higher order thinking and reasoning in college students. Their cognitive development proceeds from dualism to multiplism to relativism and eventually to commitment. That essentially is how I believe psychotherapy training should proceed – along the natural capacity of cognitive development.

w.d.   I'll encourage you to be your own critic. What's wrong with your own approach to training?

j.n.   Psychotherapy programmes committed to integrative training can expect to encounter obstacles. These come in many guises: the content itself, faculty prejudices and student resistances.

One prevalent complaint heard about integration is that there is just 'too much to know' and 'you can't do it all' during the available time. Faculty complain of insufficient time to present the material, and students complain of the resulting information overload. There remains in any training programme an inherent conflict between depth and breadth. An indisputable disadvantage of aiming to establish competence in multiple psychotherapy systems is that it will require more and longer training than establishing competency in a single system. Integrative therapists, similar to bilingual children and switch hitters in baseball, may be delayed initially in the acquisition of skills and, consequently, are more apt to feel frustrated. But there is some evidence to suggest that multiple viewpoints stimulate and maintain their interest.

Another difficulty is that various therapy systems thrive on differences and practitioners are invested in their uniqueness. The narrow and inflexible curriculum of some psychotherapy training programmes reflect their progenitor's prejudices. Private allegiances lead to over-representation, if not domination, of one or two models of psychotherapy at the expense of integration. An integrative training programme will require substantial support from the faculty, especially if we are to hire non-like minded members of the faculty.

w.d.   Your model really depends on faculty being committed to this model?

j.n.   Well, at least being committed to an informed pluralism, a training programme which will stimulate students to achieve competence in more than one therapy system.

Turning to student resistance, one frustration for many psychotherapy trainees is that their education often consists of indoctrination rather than education. Success in such programmes is frequently incumbent on the trainee adopting, or appearing to adopt, the prevailing viewpoint. They then can experience considerable difficulty in overcoming their loyalty and lethargy. Their 'separation anxiety' from the mother theory, as I call it, can be reduced by acknowledging the validity of individual theoretical preferences and the principle that integrative training is intended to build on clinicians' strengths rather than to replace their preferences. That would hit some of the recurrent obstacles we've encountered or would expect.

w.d. It seems to me that the forum for much bringing together of what students learn is clinical supervision. What are your views on how supervision is conducted in the light of what you've been saying about your ideal training model?

j.n. Let me tackle your broad question by making some generic observations on clinical supervision and then offering a few specific recommendations on supervision of integrative or eclectic therapy.

As a preface, clinical supervision, integrative or otherwise, is as complex and demanding as it gets. Supervision must incorporate and balance multiple focuses: the patient's need for competent treatment, the student's immediate comfort, the student's long-term development, the training programme's need for student evaluation, the supervisor's need to be viewed favourably, and so forth. Supervision is the most challenging professional activity of my day.

The emphasis is to be placed squarely on how to think rather than on what to think. This modified focus engenders informed pluralism and self-evolving clinical styles, in contrast to young disciples or mindless imitators.

One more general comment. For me, the supervisory relationship is a process of mutual exploration and exchange with an enquiring colleague. We should not abdicate our professional responsibilities nor deny differences in knowledge and power between ourselves and students, of course. None the less, supervisors can create a collaborative relationship and a holding environment that encourages trainees to express their insecurities and to disagree respectfully. A critical question that guides me is, 'Will trainees be able to present what makes them look bad or only what makes them look good?'

Now, more specifically, on to prescriptive supervision. Just as I ask students to try to be prescriptive in their clinical work, I, too, try to match supervision to their unique needs and clinical strategies. The therapists I supervise are far too diverse and their needs too heterogeneous to provide the identical supervision experience to each and everyone of them. Prescriptive supervision obviously takes into account numerous trainee variables. The challenge is to determine the variables to attend to. My answer is a bit complex and perhaps obsessive, but it makes sense to me.

w.d.   And what are those variables on which you base your supervision stance?

j.n.   Primarily the student's therapy approach, clinical experience and cognitive style (see Norcross 1988b).

The first is the therapy approach that the student is conducting. Within certain limits, the 'how' of supervision should parallel the 'what' of supervision. In other words, the supervision approach should mirror the therapeutic method. When the supervisee's treatment approach entails verbal, insight-oriented work, supervision profitably explores the student's counter-transference reactions to both patient and supervisor. By the same token, didactic instruction and role-playing in the supervision hour are especially congruent with more behavioural, action-oriented approaches.

The second guideline in prescriptive supervision is to match the student level of clinical experience. The developmental needs of clinical supervisees shift over the course of their training. Developmental models suggest that different supervisory styles will be differentially effective for trainees at varying levels of experience and there is some fairly good research to support this view. Beginning students are most interested in the acquisition of specific interviewing and therapy techniques; advanced practicum students are more inclined toward the development of alternative formulations; and later students tend to be most intrigued by the examination of personal dynamics affecting therapy. In oversimplified terms, students move from techniques to knowledge to self, a sequence that I often perceive among psychotherapy clients as well. Thus, the goal of supervision is to parallel the developmental stage of the trainee.

The third and final prescriptive guideline is the student's cognitive complexity, which includes a degree of self-initiative, ability to generate concepts and tolerance for ambiguity. Students high in conceptual development benefit more from a self-directed instructional approach, while those lower in conceptual development perform better with externally oriented and controlled training. To put this concretely, with some supervisees I feel more like a Rogerian resource person than a teacher, whereas with others I feel like a classroom teacher with whom the student expects and probably needs to have a very structured supervision. That's a long answer, but as you have discovered, my mind is chock full of complex and integrative ideas. Maybe that should be the subtitle of this book!

w.d.   Let's be a bit more specific about that. What specific practices have you found helpful in the supervision of integrative therapy?

j.n.   There are many. I'll share a few that are supported by a few sprinkles of empirical evidence and many years of supervision experience, not only mine. For one, despite their initial anxiety, our students appreciate reliance on more than their edited verbal reports about what transpired during psychotherapy contacts. Research suggests verbatim recordings and direct observation are superior methods to reconstructed tales of therapy heroics.

A second, heartily recommended supervision strategy is to use a wide variety of pedagogical methods. Structure should follow function. As the situation dictates, supervision can involve didactic presentations, reading assignments, open-ended discussions, personal modelling, experiential activities, video demonstrations, case examples and mini-case conferences. I do not see it simply as a face-to-face chat. The needs of supervisees are too diverse to keep it to a single unitary model. Two techniques that have proven quite effective in expanding my own theoretical horizons are, first, formulating the same case from disparate theoretical perspectives, as in *Therapy Wars*, and, second, conducting co-supervision with an invited colleague. The latter can be quite challenging, even upsetting, but it does teach us the lessons of pluralism and modesty.

A third method that I – and other supervisors – have found useful is to examine the recurrence of parallels between supervision and psychotherapy. These parallel processes can take many forms. In one manifestation, trainees may behave in supervision in a way that is similar to how their patient behaves in psychotherapy. In another manifestation, the dynamics between supervisee and supervisor may mimic those of the therapeutic relationship. Trainees bring similar interpersonal and defensive patterns to all relationships, psychotherapy and supervision included. When these repetitive relationship patterns are addressed in supervision, the trainee's performance can be enhanced in all interpersonal pursuits, including but not limited to psychotherapy. When I recommend this third method, psychoanalysts immediately recognize it as something they have been doing for years. However, I believe it is under-utilized by supervisors from other theoretical persuasions.

w.d.   In some of your recent work, John, you heavily criticize the paucity of systematic evaluation of clinical training. Can you elaborate on this please?

J.N.   The competence of our graduates and the adequacy of clinical training typically are assumed rather than verified. We have found that most clinical training programmes have not evaluated systematically their impact on trainees nor their trainees' impact on clients (see Stevenson and Norcross 1987 for a review). Jay Haley has said that the most curious aspect of training is that student success or failure with their training cases is never examined.

Evaluation of our training is probably the most overlooked issue in training. The need to evaluate training and process has become particularly intense at this time of declining federal support, shrinking job market, and increasing demands for demonstration of professional competence.

In 1982 a Task Force of the American Psychological Association (APA 1982) concluded that the first step in developing ways to assess the effects of education and training would be to survey training programmes in clinical psychology, including internship programmes, about their ways of assessing their own students and trainees. The task force's recommendation foreshadowed our survey efforts and results. John Stevenson and I (Norcross and Stevenson 1984; Stevenson and Norcross 1985; Stevenson, Norcross, King and Tobin 1984) conducted several national studies of training clinics, graduate programmes, and internship programmes concerning the procedures, practices and problems associated with clinical training evaluation. Without exception, results of those studies indicated that current clinical evaluation practices heavily favour student-focused, impressionistically collected, qualitatively oriented sources of evidence to judge their training enterprise. Across categories, informal and qualitative procedures were utilized the most; formal and quantitative procedures the least.

W.D.   Let's take the ordinary trainer who doesn't have access to research facilities. How would you suggest that he or she go about evaluating their training work?

J.N.   Systematic evaluation of training does not require access to mainframe computers, external funding or multivariate statistics. Although there is certainly a genuine need for formal comparative designs, more urgent and more useful are local, critical examinations of training. Our research consistently documents that training can be directly improved by formative feedback from ongoing low-cost evaluation.

We asked clinical directors to nominate two evaluation methods they would recommend to other programmes. I'll base my specific recommendations on their collective thousand years of experience in these matters. They recommend: structured and anonymous student feedback on programme components; student evaluations of supervisor or faculty in a structured and anonymous way which includes quantitative ratings; and post-training follow-up of students including their satisfactions, their certification rates, their employment status, their diplomate status and the like. Finally, as previously mentioned, programme directors endorse use of competency-based and manual-driven training in which students do not complete the programme until their proficiency, by some recognized standard, has been documented. This training emphasis builds in an ongoing evaluation component.

W.D.   John, do you have any final words on the evaluation of clinical training before we finish?

J.N.   Yes. Get started! Evaluation should be a high priority. Waiting for the single, universally approved measure of competence or the ideal research design is ill-advised. Training questions are scientifically interesting and profoundly pragmatic. It is high time to build some evidence and improve our training. Get started now.

W.D.   Let's finish by combining your interests in psychotherapy integration and clinical training. Do you see any connection?

J.N.   Definitely. The introduction of an integrative approach to clinical work compounds the training enterprise. Single, 'pure' systems of psychotherapy markedly reduce the range of clinical observations and treatment possibilities. Now, with these perceptual blinders loosened, a broader range of formulations and interventions must be carefully considered. Not only must students become aware of the relative indications for matching patient and treatment but also they, in many cases, must become competent in offering multiple therapy modalities. Both are unprecedented training objectives in the history of psychotherapy.

While I am optimistic about the prospects of integrative training, my intention is not necessarily to produce card-carrying, flag-waving 'integrative' psychotherapists. Instead the goal is to educate therapists to think and, perhaps, to behave integratively – openly, synthetically, but critically – in their clinical pursuits.

I firmly believe that it is *in*appropriate to demand that students adopt any single metatheoretical perspective, integrative or otherwise. Each practitioner should develop an individual clinical style within his or her chosen perspective. The hope is that, in Halleck's (1978) words, students will 'approach our patients with open minds and a relentless commitment to study and confront the complexities of human behavior'.

| 7

| SELF-CHANGE

WINDY DRYDEN In this interview, John, I'd like to focus our attention on an area in which you've done a lot of research, that is, self-change. First of all what is self-change and how does it differ from the concept of self-help?

JOHN NORCROSS Self-initiated change, or its shorthand, self-change, is a concerted effort to alter one's cognitions, emotions or behaviours without external professional assistance. Treatment-facilitated change or what we call therapy-change, refers to change attempted with the aid of professional treatment.

Self-help has a parental, pejorative connotation to it: 'help yourself along until something meaningful or someone professional can treat you'. Self-change, by contrast, is proactive, life-enhancing; self-help sounds reactive, accepting the dreadful circumstances. But people can and frequently do change them-selves in life-enhancing directions on their own without or before professional treatment.

W.D. You have conducted research on both laypersons and psycho-therapists' self-change. Let's first look at the self-change of laypersons. How prevalent are their attempts to initiate change on their own and how durable are their attempts to do so?

J.N. Prevalence of self-change is quite high. The vast majority of distressed individuals do *not* bring their problems to mental health professionals. They cope with their difficulties through their own adaptive capacities or with the help of friends, clergy or others who may provide counsel. Although 15–19 per cent of the American adult population will have a diagnosable mental disorder at any given time, only 3 per cent receive specialized mental health services in any given year. Overall, only about one-quarter of those suffering from a clinically significant disorder have *ever* been in treatment. That leaves three-quarters of the population on their own.

A famous 1957 nation-wide survey (Gurin, Veroff and Feld 1960) and a 1976 follow-up study (Veroff, Douvan and Kulka 1981a; 1981b) determined that practically everyone coped with problems on their own before or without professional assistance. When they did seek assistance, most did *not* choose psychotherapists. Instead, they typically turned to non-mental health professionals: 42 per cent turned to clergy, 29 per cent to physicians, and 6 per cent to lawyers. Common sense and Emory Cowen (1982) suggest hairdressers and bartenders also offer invaluable service in this respect.

Our unfortunate proclivity to focus on formal psychotherapy rather than natural self-initiated attempts leads to a devaluation of self-change. Successful self-change is probably far more common and successful than heretofore anticipated. In part, people who change themselves do not generally seek professional assistance. Our views of the intractability of certain behavioural problems have been moulded largely by the self-selected, hard-core group of people who, unable or unwilling to help themselves, go to psychotherapists for help, thereby becoming the available subjects for investigations. Additionally the self-esteem, legal mandate and economic survival of many psychotherapists are contingent on their unique ability to help people. Evidence for the efficacy of self-change is threatening and frequently dismissed.

As it is, the self-change success of tobacco smoking, moderate alcohol abuse, and mild to moderate depression is fairly good. If self-reports are to be trusted, many self-changers experience improvement rates impressive even by professional standards. Not everyone changes, of course, but most do, and substantially on their own (see also Taylor 1983).

w.d.   What are the limits of self-initiated change attempts by laypersons?

j.n.   As with any behaviour change effort, self-change has its contra-indications and limitations. Two obvious constraints are severe mental disorders – in which energy level or reality testing are disrupted – and forced change. Self-change, by definition, is intentional, not forced.

In addition, there are a number of limitations in written self-change materials, which I call the 'three unables'. The first is unable to understand. Some people will distort or misunderstand the change principles presented in a book no matter how clearly or concretely presented. In the minority of cases, this may be due to intellectual, visual or memory limitations. But in the majority of cases, the inability to understand is the ubiquitous problem of selective perception.

Second is unable to apply. One thing we should remember is that psychotherapy provides a systematic check on whether the message is being truly understood and applied. In self-change books, this is not possible. After we give public presentations on self-change, a few members of the audience will come forward to compliment us on our approach, tell us how much it makes sense and pulls everything together for them. But they then wonder aloud how all of this applies to their specific problem. This wonderment implies conceptual understanding without practical application.

The third unable is the inability to comply. Perhaps people are able to understand self-change methods and begin to tentatively apply them. But as quickly as they began, they stop. This common pattern of inadequate maintenance probably indicates a need for professional assistance.

W.D.   You mentioned self-help materials. Do people read and benefit from these books or do they just buy them, shelve them and that's the end of it?

J.N.   There is great variation. I suspect it's like asking whether clients purchase and benefit from psychotherapy. There is a persistent danger of the $7 fix. People run out, grab a paperback, read two pages, then shelve it with a dozen other self-help books.

The evidence is fairly clear that people with some college education routinely purchase self-help materials. How successful they are has rarely been systematically investigated. In fact, the American Psychological Association commissioned a task force on this issue several years ago and is now reconstituting it, because so many books are published every year and so few of them have ever scientifically tracked the success of people using the book in question. Self-change books are usually published without benefit of any empirical outcome research.

By contrast, Jim Prochaska of the University of Rhode Island, Carlo DiClemente of the University of Houston, and I are putting the finishing touches on a book that has a decade of empirical research on self-change behind it.

W.D.   One concept that stands out to me in your self-change materials is that of stages of change. Could you describe this particular construct and why it's so important in the self-change literature?

J.N.   In the tradebook that Jim, Carlo and I are finishing, the stages of change are the organizing element. Following an introduction to the transtheoretical model, we devote one chapter to each stage – defining the stage, identifying common resistances at that point, demonstrating the positive processes of change, and describing how to establish conducive helping relationships specific to that stage.

In both psychotherapy and self-change, we have found people transverse a series of stages: precontemplation, contemplation, action and maintenance.

Precontemplation is the stage in which people are not intending to change their behaviour. They are unaware or underaware of their problems. As G. K. Chesterton once said, 'It isn't that they can't see the solution. It is that they can't see the problem.' Their families, friends, neighbours and employees, of course, are well aware of the problem. When precontemplators present for psychotherapy, they usually do so because of pressure from others. Typically they feel coerced into changing by a spouse who threatens to leave, an employer who threatens to dismiss them, or parents who threaten to disown them.

The therapeutic challenge in working with precontemplators is to move beyond their defences. One of my favourite anti-defence advertisements is from the American Heart Association. It reads 'Millions of Americans are suffering from a serious health problem. Denial.'

Contemplation is the stage in which people become aware that a problem exists and begin to seriously consider overcoming it. Although contemplators think about changing their behaviour, they haven't made the commitments to take action. And we know people can remain stuck in the contemplation stage for long periods.

The essence of the contemplation stage is beautifully communicated in an incident related by the counsellor, Alfred Benjamin (1987). He was walking home one evening when a stranger approached him and enquired as to the whereabouts of a certain street. Benjamin pointed it out to the stranger and provided specific instructions. After readily understanding and accepting the instructions, the stranger began to walk in the opposite direction that Benjamin had indicated. Benjamin said, 'You are headed in the wrong direction.' The stranger replied, 'Yes, I know.

I am not quite ready yet.' This is contemplation: knowing where you want to go, but not quite ready yet.

w.d.   That brings us to the action stage.

j.n.   Right. Action is the stage in which people modify their behaviour, experiences and environment in order to overcome their problems. Action is the busiest stage and requires considerable commitment of time and energy. Changes made in the action stage tend to be the most visible and receive the greatest external recognition.

As a result, people often erroneously equate the entire change process with the action stage. If they do so, they overlook the requisite work that prepares them for action. Professionals frequently design excellent action-oriented programmes to help people change, but then are disappointed when only a small percentage of troubled people register or when large numbers drop out of the programme after signing up.

Maintenance is the stage in which people work to prevent relapse and consolidate their gains attained during action. Traditionally, maintenance was viewed as a static change. But we now know maintenance is a continuation, not an absence of change. As is also well documented, most self-changers do *not* maintain their gains on their first attempt. With smoking, for example, successful self-changers make an average of five to six action attempts before they become long-term maintainers. Many New Year's resolvers report five or more consecutive pledges before maintaining their behavioural goal for at least six months (see e.g. Norcross, Ratzin and Payne 1989).

As I describe these stages of change, psychotherapists immediately recognize them for their clinical relevance. But then they have a recurring question about all this stuff: 'So what? We know clients differ in readiness to change.'

The answer to this 'so what' question is that the stages of change variable has proven to be the single *best* predictor of success in self-change and therapy-change across a series of studies. Compared to a host of variables from diverse theoretical origins, the stages concept out-performs the other variables in showing who stays in treatment and who progresses in behaviour change, be it self-initiated or therapy facilitated.

w.d.   Originally there was a fifth stage called 'decision' that got edited out of the model because the research did not indicate that it was an independent stage.

J.N.   It's a bit more complex than that. The decision stage was
discarded because decision-making is such a brief stage which
made it difficult to capture in research studies. But between
contemplation and action, there is obviously a decisional and
preparation process that occurs when people decide to go and
change their behaviour.

W.D.   Do you think that its omission from the model emphasizes the
notion that self-change really involves a continuing responsibility
to behaviour change?

J.N.   You will probably be pleased to hear that the transtheoretical
model has another stage called preparation which emphasizes
exactly your point: the continuing responsibility, the ongoing
decisional processes, weighing the pros and cons, and remember-
ing that you are responsible for initiating the change and maintaining it. Research clarity led to its elimination, but clinically we all
know it's there.

W.D.   Could we consider in detail the major change processes that
you discussed in the self-change model? Which of these processes
are the most effective at which stages of change?

J.N.   That really is the crux of the matter, isn't it? Probably the most
direct implication of our research is to assess the stage of client
readiness for change and tailor interventions accordingly.
Although this step may be taken by many experienced clinicians, a
more explicit model would enhance efficient, integrative and
prescriptive treatment plans.

Furthermore, this step is rarely taken in a conscious and
meaningful way by self-changers in the natural environment. As
we interview self-changers in our studies, vague notions of
willpower and mysticism dominate their perspectives on self-
change. Common examples are 'I can't do it', 'I tried everything',
or 'I simply don't have what it takes – the courage or the moral
fibre'. Jim Prochaska once said that if people knew as little about
their automobiles as they did about self-change, there would only
be three automobiles operating in the world.

We found that matching therapy to client's pre-treatment stage of
change will afford more progress and will better serve clinicians
and clients alike. For instance, treating contemplators together and
helping them move one stage at a time through the preparation
stage into action is more effective than trying to rush them directly
through action to maintenance.

Individuals in precontemplation do little on their own. There's little hard data on how to help them into contemplation, but the key is to educate, persuade and tickle their defences, as I call it. The precontemplation stage is the foremost challenge for contemporary psychotherapists – how to help someone who insists there is nothing wrong.

Individuals in the contemplation stage are most open to consciousness-raising techniques, such as observations, confrontations and interpretations. They are much more likely to use bibliotherapy and other educational techniques. As contemplators become more conscious of themselves and the nature of their problems, they are more likely to re-evaluate themselves both affectively and cognitively. A process which we call self-re-evaluation.

w.d.   And during action?

j.n.   During the action stage, individuals act from a sense of self-liberation or committed will-power. They believe that they have the autonomy to alter their lives in central ways. People in action must also be effective with behavioural processes, such as counter-conditioning and stimulus control, to modify the stimuli that prompt relapse.

Successful maintenance then builds on each of the preceding processes. Specific preparation for maintenance entails an assessment of the conditions under which a person is likely to relapse and the development of alternative responses. I find Marlatt and Gordon's (1985) relapse prevention work compelling in this regard. Continuing to apply counter-conditioning and stimulus control is most effective when it is based on the conviction that maintaining change supports a self-concept that is highly valued by oneself and significant others.

A recent illustration will give you a sense of the range of stages that self-changers are in at any one time. In a survey of smokers at a worksite, David Abrams and colleagues (1988) at Brown Medical School determined that fewer than 10 per cent of cigarette smokers were prepared for action, approximately 30 per cent were in the contemplation stage, and 60 per cent were in the precontemplation stage. If these data hold for other problems, then professionals offering action-oriented programs are mistreating the majority of people.

w.d.   What are the most common mistakes that people make in changing on their own?

j.n.   We have interviewed dozens upon dozens of unsuccessful self-changers who were genuinely invested in changing themselves but who were unwittingly misintegrating the processes and stages of change. We have observed two frequent mismatches. First, some self-changers rely primarily on change processes most indicated for the contemplation stage – consciousness raising, self-re-evaluation – while they are in the action stage. They try to modify behaviours by becoming more aware, a common criticism of classical psychoanalysis: insight alone does not necessarily bring about behaviour change.

The second major mismatch is relying primarily on self-change processes most indicated for the action state – reinforcement management, counter-conditioning, stimulus control – without the requisite awareness and preparation provided by the contemplation stage. They try to modify behaviour without awareness, a common criticism of behaviourism: overt action without insight is likely to be temporary change.

W.D.   How do you combine psychotherapy and client's self-change in psychotherapy?

J.N.   Psychotherapy patients, almost without exception, are also self-changers in that they have attempted to change before seeking treatment. Their pre-treatment self-change is typically insufficient, but in many cases was partially effective. It is not, therefore, a battle between self-change and therapy-change.

Incidentally, in this regard, one clinical hint I give to my students is to ask clients during the first interview what they have tried on their own. Therapists who unwittingly advise patients to try what they've already tried unsuccessfully find their clients not returning. Common sense perhaps, but many students forget that clients have attempted numerous methods before presenting for formal treatment.

The relationship between self-change and therapy-change is one I characterize as a friendly alliance. When one, like self-change, can function well without the other, all the better. When one requires an assistance, as with self-change needing a boost from psychotherapy, they operate as allies.

Psychotherapists are acutely aware of the necessary and mutual facilitation of therapy-change and self-change. A panel of psychotherapy experts (Prochaska and Norcross 1982) estimated that, in general, 62 per cent of all behaviour change is determined by the clients' efforts and 36 per cent is determined by the therapists' efforts. The challenge, therefore, is to integrate self-change and therapy-change for maximum synergistic benefit.

The overarching strategy is for psychotherapists to focus in treatment on the change processes not currently under clients' control and simultaneously to encourage clients to work with change processes that are available through their self-control. In one of our research studies, Jim Prochaska and I (Norcross and Prochaska 1988; Norcross, Prochaska and Hambrecht, in press) discovered that psychotherapists relied more on helping relationships and medications when treating clients then when treating themselves. Why? Probably because these interventions are usually provided or recommended by a professional; clients cannot easily manage the availability of medication and support by themselves. Thus, therapists emphasize these processes in treatment precisely because they are under their control and try to instruct and facilitate clients using processes of change under their control, a far more mutual and powerful means of integrating the two.

w.d.   Perhaps we can make this more concrete by a clinical example which shows the meshing between psychotherapy and client self-change.

j.n.   Sure. I recently saw a 50-ish-year-old married man, let's call him Roland, referred by a neurologist for psychological treatment of chronic pain. I recall this gentlemen distinctly because the first words out of Roland's mouth were: 'Well, what the hell do you think you're going to do for me?' His angry tone belied a deep sense of frustration and apathy. With a little prodding, Roland went on to relate a ten-year history of unremitting pain and resulting distress, largely depression and anxiety. His physicians had tried virtually everything, including various medications, steroid injections, back surgery, professional hypnosis, electrical nerve stimulators and several experimental techniques. By now, Roland was convinced that he could do, in his words, 'not a damn thing' to help himself. The well-intentioned promises of medical magic and their constant failure had drained him of whatever personal resources he once possessed. In this vein, I like B. F. Skinner's (1986) warning that over-reliance on formal treatment deprives people of their autonomy and of the confidence in their everyday remedies.

Anyway, to his demanding question came my answer, 'Not much'. Roland was surprised and chortled, but I went on to tell him that I could help him find ways of improving his life with pain. Now he was interested and, his wife, mute to this point, also became alert. This is the standard cognitive-behavioural treatment plan for chronic pain – 'We realize you have pain refractory to your doctor's best methods. I cannot eliminate it. But, if you like, I will show you and your wife methods of enhancing your behaviour on your own.' Like many people, Roland and his wife saw professional treatment as an entire substitute for self-change. It's a classic example of dualistic, either/or thinking: either surgery or nothing; either therapy-change or self-change.

In therapy, Roland responded well to a caring, disclosing and honest alliance, a therapeutic relationship he had not experienced with his physicians. Clinicians experienced in chronic pain encounter this pattern frequently – a physician becomes guilty, frustrated and angry by not being able to alleviate the patient's pain. In Roland's case, his chronic pain complaints had alienated those around him, leaving him with little support. I emphasized our collaborative relationship in part because Roland was finding it difficult to obtain interpersonal nurturance himself. By the same token, Roland later agreed to an antidepressant to combat several of the biological or vegetative components of his depression. Clients obviously cannot order prescription medication for themselves.

At the same time, there were a number of change processes potentially under Roland's direction. Exercise, relaxation and cognitive restructuring are processes that are fairly easily taught and brought under self-control. Even reward can be self-managed or mate-managed by Roland's wife. With knowledge and instruction, Roland and his family were able to successfully employ these processes. In this and most cases, the client's work and the therapist's work together produced a positive outcome that either alone could not have achieved. This, I believe, is the lesson of self-change plus therapy change.

w.d.   One of the ways that psychotherapy has been criticized, in the light of what you have said, is that it focuses too much on the content of what clients say and not enough on the process of helping clients to initiate and maintain self-change processes. Would you say that is a fair criticism?

j.n.   I certainly agree. There are a number of ongoing efforts to clarify this content–process distinction. The transtheoretical model of change is relatively content free in that regard.

w.d.   You have conducted a series of longitudinal studies on self-change success, particularly examining relapse. What are the long-term success rates and what predicts success?

J.N.   In drawing together our studies over the past twelve years for the book, we surprised ourselves to discover how many self-changers we followed over the years. Jim Prochaska and Carlo DiClemente began by interviewing 200 people who had tried to quit smoking, some successfully, some unsuccessfully, some with professional help, but most on their own. For two years, they then followed a sample of 1,000 people struggling to quit smoking by themselves. Since that time, we have collected data from 800 people attempting to lose weight either on their own or in professional weight-control programmes. We tracked more than 1,000 people suffering from emotional distress and comparable numbers of psychotherapists, as we discussed in an earlier interview, told us how they attempt to help their clients overcome the same distress. We also looked at more than 1,000 individuals in inpatient treatment, including 400 alcoholics. Most recently, students and I tracked the self-change experiences of 200 New Year's resolvers over a two-year span.

Let me take New Year resolutions as an example. In the United States, resolutions have become an annual tradition for over one-half of American adults and consist primarily of smoking cessation, weight loss and alcohol reduction. Is the same true here [Britain]?

W.D.   I believe so, yes.

J.N.   Resolutions thus provide a prime opportunity to examine the maintenance of naturally occurring efforts to modify behaviour. Our study prospectively tracked the self-change attempts over this two-year span. Of the participants 77 per cent maintained their vow for one week, 55 per cent for one month, 40 per cent for six months, but only 19 per cent for a full two years (Norcross, Ratzin and Payne 1989). This pattern is consistent with the familiar survival curve and relapse rates in the addictions.

Stage of change and self-efficacy prospectively predicted successful outcome in both the short run and long run. Throughout the study, successful resolvers were found to use significantly more cognitive and behavioural strategies and less self-blame and wishful thinking than unsuccessful resolvers. Again, the stages of change instrument predicted the best and, in this particular study, self-efficacy came a close second. Fans of Albert Bandura should like that one.

W.D.   What are the major lessons that we can learn from the research about relapse?

J.N. We try to show how these hard-lost battles can inform subsequent self-change efforts. My grandmother was fond of saying, 'If you have to fail or make a mistake, at least learn from it.'

The first lesson is that few self-changers make it the first time around. Most of us have already learned from experience that we are not likely to overcome our problems on our first attempt. Therapy clients and self-changers should be aware of that. Clinical research confirms this: only 20 per cent of the population permanently overcomes long-standing problems on the first try. Put another way, 60–80 per cent will relapse within six months of taking action to change a serious behavioural problem.

The second lesson is that a lapse is not a relapse. In overcoming problems, people slip back at times to the old ways. But a temporary lapse does not mean that you have to relapse. There are many people, as Marlatt and Gordon (1985) have reported, who believe that a slip makes a fall. As soon as they have a lapse, they give up and find they have relapsed. This phenomenon, known as the Abstinence Violation Effect, afflicts many people. I like to use a datum from our New Year's resolution study: successful resolvers over two years suffered an average of fourteen lapses, but obviously did not let a slip become a fall.

A third lesson is to prepare for the major causes of relapse – emotional distress and social pressure. Researchers consistently find that distress is involved in about 60 per cent of relapse situations for alcohol, drugs, smoking and eating problems. Self-changers should build in a relapse prevention plan that takes into account these high risk situations.

And a final lesson is to put your learning into action. Many therapists and self-changers have excellent ideas, but they aren't useful if you don't put them to work. Someone once said, 'Good ideas eventually deteriorate into hard work.' One of the crucial lessons we have learned from thousands of self-changers is that far too many people get stuck in contemplation. Previous relapses should prepare you for subsequent self-changes, ready to base future action on informed and proven change principles. Learn from your relapse; that's it in a nutshell.

W.D. You mentioned earlier that you've done research on therapists' self-change efforts and we've alluded to that in the interview on the person of the therapist. But more specifically, how do psychotherapists' self-change efforts differ from those of laypersons?

J.N. We've conducted two studies precisely on that question. What do the mental health 'experts' offer themselves and how is that different from self-change of non-therapists? Our studies, which have involved hundreds of psychotherapists, revealed a number of intriguing differences. Psychotherapists use helping relationships significantly more frequently than laypersons. This disparity probably attests to the interpersonal emphasis of the profession. Psychotherapists also employ more stimulus control and counter-conditioning, concrete behavioural strategies for action.

On the other hand, it would be naive and presumptuous to assume that psychotherapists simply do more of everything than laypersons. In fact, laypersons report significantly more frequent use of three strategies: Self-Re-evaluation, Wishful Thinking, and Self-Blame. These are all alike in focusing on the self, as opposed to other people and all involved internal cognitive strategies. In an ironic twist, laypersons get more caught up in their heads than shrinks!

Two traditional misperceptions about psychotherapists is that they only talk about life (yak, yak, yak) and that they are only concerned about individuals (me, me, me). Our findings contradict this stereotype. When it comes to self-change anyway, psychotherapists use more action-oriented processes in place of seemingly unending talk. They also rely heavily on interpersonal relationships in place of self-contained individualism. And clinicians are also experienced enough to know that wishing and blaming are not viable solutions to life's problems.

w.d.   What are the clinical implications of what you have just said, John?

j.n.   While additional research is required on these matters, I am convinced that seasoned psychotherapists have learned important lessons from their clinical work which extend to their personal lives. Several of these lessons for psychotherapy are: blend methods from diverse therapies, emphasize the human element, minimize self-blame, avoid the single technique, translate insight into action, and promote cognitive and experiential learning on a broad front. That's my kind of prescription for everybody's self-change.

w.d.   At this point readers probably can't get out of their mind one particular question: How do you go about helping a precontemplator move out of that stage and into the contemplation stage? Because the clinicians whom I've spoken to indicate that's a major problem they face in their clinical practice.

J.N.   Well, I wish we had definite recommendations. I would employ them myself. Precontemplation is what I call a double whammy. Patients in this stage are the most resistant, and research on this stage is the most meagre. So what follows are some gleanings from research and probably more my clinical experience in pondering this challenge.

Precontemplators are defensive, resist awareness and change. These defences create dilemmas for the psychotherapist and concerned people. One is whether people can have a problem if they are not aware that they have a problem. Put another way, who decides whether a particular behavioural pattern is a problem or a preference? Another dilemma has to do with whether or not it is ethical to try to help someone change who doesn't want to change. Put another way, should we mind our business when someone we care about has a problem but does not perceive it as a problem? Of course, these two dilemmas do not arise for people in other stages of change who are aware of their disorder and wish to modify it at some point.

One answer to these dilemmas has been to wait until the problems become so severe that they are undeniable. With alcoholics, to take an example, there has been a public myth that holds that alcoholics will not be ready to change until they hit the bottom of the barrel. However, this answer poses unnecessary risks. It's painful to watch people deteriorate, the problems get harder to treat successfully as they get more severe, the dysfunction worsens and so on. So my first answer would be not to try to wait until precontemplators hit bottom. Sometimes we do not have alternatives, but it is unrealistic and almost unethical not to make a sincere effort to do something. We certainly would not do so with medical disorders.

Our research shows that there are three potent processes of change to move precontemplators into the contemplation stage. These are consciousness-raising, social liberation and helping relationships. However, I hasten to clarify that when someone refuses to sit and listen, these processes won't be much good. Consciousness-raising is essentially the principle that knowledge is power. To change intentionally we must become conscious of our self-defeating defences in the precontemplation stage. Becoming more aware of how we get on in our own way. Freud was the first to recognize that overcoming our compulsions begins by analysing our resistance to change.

The second broad strategy is social liberation – helping people to distinguish between pressure and persuasion. Social liberation involves changes in the environment which lead to more alternatives and choices being open to the individual. We have quit smoking days and public education campaigns and so forth. Creating no smoking sections in airplanes, restaurants and workplaces are common examples of change designed to free people from smoke or the temptation to smoke. I ask my precontemplation clients whether they experienced these as influence or coercion. We deal in great depth with their high reactance to change and that a friendly influence is interpreted invariably as a coercive power tactic. This is particularly true in conjoint marital sessions when, as is frequently the case, one partner will present in the contemplation stage and the other, stereotypically the husband, will be dragged in as a precontemplator.

The third process to move precontemplators into the contemplation stage is probably the most urgent one and that is the helping relationship. We request clients to ask others to identify their defences against recognizing the problems. To follow-up on the conjoint marital example, we ask people they feel close to, be it a spouse, a friend at work or a neighbour, to identify how the precontemplator defends against recognizing difficulties in their marriage.

W.D.   One aspect of this might be the work done on people known as enablers, somehow wanting to make life better for the person with an addiction. But in doing so, the enabler almost deprives the person from recognizing the consequences of their problem.

J.N.   Yes. The enabler or the co-dependant maintains the patient's defences against the recognition and consequences of the addiction.

Another clinical guideline about precontemplation is to remind family members and clinicians to help move the precontemplator one stage at a time. Our goal is to move them into contemplation, into awareness, not to immediately change their behaviour. A simple clarification can reduce massive resistance and enhance progress. Premature pushes into the action stage, demanding that clients change their behaviour immediately, often backfire.

One of our workshop participants recently related a classic illustration of premature action. She was a newly married, middle-aged wife imploring her new husband to kick his fifteen-year-old cigar habit. She would take every opportunity to remind him of its health dangers and the prospects of self-change. The husband, a dyed-in-the-wool precontemplator uninterested in modifying anything, was able to ignore this 'constant bantering' until his wife escalated her suggestions into a demand. He then reluctantly registered for a smoking-cessation programme with all the probability of changing as catching fish in a toilet bowl. He dropped out after two meetings, full of self-righteousness and condemnation of others. He had set himself up for premature action in order to fail this time and to prevent a next time. She had set herself up for failure by pushing her husband too quickly from precontemplation into action. I see this pattern time and time again in clinical encounters.

w.D.   Right. Let's finish up with this question of how you distinguish between problems and preferences.

J.N.   We begin to distinguish between problems and preferences in ourselves and our clients by asking a series of questions.

First, are you defensive about a particular behaviour pattern? Do you become self-conscious if people are talking about possible problems? Do you turn the page or change the channel when there is discussion about one of your behaviours? If someone suggests that your behaviour may be a problem, do you resent it, resist it, or tell them you appreciate their concern? Ironically if you are not in the precontemplation stage and do not have a problem, then there is no need to become defensive. You should be able to recognize people's feedback as signs of caring rather than attempts to control.

Second, are you well-informed about your behaviour? If you are not defensive about your behaviour, you should be able to read articles on the topic with keen interest. Do you know what experts say about your behaviour or do you say defensively, 'What do experts know?'

A third question: Are you aware of the short-term and long-term consequences of your behaviour? Can you imagine the long-term consequences of your behaviour and feel good about your personal choices? If you smoke, for example, can you imagine developing lung cancer and feeling pleased and proud about your choice to smoke? Can you fantasize your children continuing to live with you as adults, unable to leave home because they are too dependent on you, and feel right about how you are raising them? Precontemplators become uncomfortable or defensive when asked to vividly imagine the long-term consequences of their behaviour.

And fourth, are you willing to take responsibility for the

long-term consequences of your behaviour? If you die from the way you live, will you accept the outcome as the natural consequences? Will you take responsibility for your own death if it is the result of the way you live?

Candid responses to these four questions can provide a good sense of whether a particular behaviour is a problem or a preference. If a person can honestly say that he or she is non-defensive, well-informed, aware of the consequences, and responsible for the long-term effects of the behaviour, then perhaps it is a preference. If, however, like most of us, he or she answered 'no' to one or more of the questions, then precontemplation is probably operative.

THE FUTURE OF
PSYCHOTHERAPY

WINDY DRYDEN   Having just edited a centennial issue of *Psychotherapy* on the future of psychotherapy (Norcross 1992), what impresses you most about our orientation to the future?

JOHN NORCROSS   That psychotherapy, as a discipline, has not been sufficiently proactive in anticipating and, more importantly, guiding the future. The literature on the future of psychotherapy consists mainly of magical wish-fulfilments and reactive laments. The former unrealistically portend greater emphasis for each of their psychotherapy systems; the latter wonder aloud about how things got so bad and how we might deal with the alleged disarrangement. From these publications, one would never surmise that the profession is seriously interested in the future of psychotherapy and genuinely committed to shaping its directions into the twenty-first century.

W.D.   Specifically what are the theoretical emphases, therapy formats, and provider groups of psychotherapy in the future according to Delphi polls?

J.N.   Every ten years – starting in 1980 – colleagues and I have attempted to identify and anticipate trends that will have a marked impact on psychotherapy. We secure the consensus of a panel of experts, representing diverse orientations and specializations, using the Delphi method.

 The Delphi method, developed in the early 1950s, was part of military research concerning the most reliable consensus of a group of experts by a series of intensive questionnaires interspersed with controlled opinion feedback. Delphi polls across a range of disciplines have indicated that consensus of an entire panel is more accurate than the best estimates of any individual expert.

The Delphi poll is a method for structuring a group communication so that the process is effective in allowing a group of individuals, as a whole, to deal with a complex problem. A panel of experts answer the same questions at least twice. In the first round the experts answer the questions anonymously and without feedback. In subsequent rounds, participants are provided with the panel members' names and their views and given the opportunity to revise their opinions in light of the group judgement. The Delphi method then facilitates consensus among experts and is particularly valuable in topical areas in which accurate information is unavailable, like the future of psychotherapy.

Our 1990 Delphi results, comprising the composite predictions of eighty-one experts, are just now available. Bear in mind that these are American experts, but I expect the trends will hold true throughout industrialized nations. As for theoretical orientations, technical eclecticism, theoretical integration, cognitive therapy and family systems therapies are hot; whereas conventional psycho-analysis, transactional analysis and existential therapy are not. As for modalities, psycho-educational classes for specific disorders, marital/couple therapy, and conjoint family therapy will be hot. Individual therapy will not.

Predictably in the light of health cost-containment measures and restrictions on mental health coverage, short-term therapy will be the wave of the future. For better or worse, long-term therapy will be limited to selected cases or wealthy clients. As for psychotherapy providers, experts foresee continuing growth of self-help groups and non-medical psychotherapists, including psychiatric nurses, social workers and clinical psychologists. By contrast, the proportion of psychotherapy provided by psychiatrists is seen as rapidly declining, part and parcel of the shrinkage and re-medicalization of psychiatry.

w.d.   What mental health applications do you see being valued in the future?

j.n.   Our intrepid observers are in agreement that psychotherapy will become more cognitive-behavioural, present centred, problem specific, and briefer as we approach the millennium. Cathartic, aversive, dynamic and long-term approaches are predicted to decrease in application and popularity. The writing is on the wall.

Consider, for example, the specific therapeutic interventions predicted to increase dramatically: self-change techniques, cognitive restructuring, problem-solving techniques, homework assignments and *in vivo* exposure. It's very clear where the experts say psychotherapy is heading, and I believe they are accurate.

As far as where John Norcross would like to see us proceed, I endorse these clinical megatrends, so to speak, as one element in a broader therapeutic repertoire. However, I am aghast at the remedicalization of psychological intervention and afraid that insistence on short-term intervention will push out indicated long-term psychotherapy.

W.D.   I am puzzled by that trend. I can understand the need to be cost effective, but there is also quite an interest in working with people with personality disorders. If we know anything about working with these kind of patients, we know that it's not brief. How could the conflicts between these two interests be resolved in the future?

J.N.   Clients with personality disorders should always have the indicated lengthier treatments available. Those who do not will probably be offered intermittent psychotherapy throughout their life cycle – brief targeted therapies to control their symptom exacerbation. This is precisely what we would clinically not want, namely attention to the burning trees (that is symptoms) while the forest (that is character) is decimated.

I would like to return briefly in our dialogue to the biological reductionism which frightens me. In the United States, President Bush has christened the 1990s the 'decade of the brain'. In the airline flight over for these interviews, I read that John Naisbitt (Naisbitt and Aburdene 1990) has identified 'the age of biology' as one of his millennial megatrends. In mental health we are already witnessing the transformation and respecialization of psychiatry into neuroscience. In fact, one of the composite predictions of the Delphi panel was that psychotropic medications will expand at the expense of psychotherapy.

One cannot argue against the pharmacological miracles of modern neuroleptics and antidepressants, of course. Nor would I devalue the contributions of neuroscience to our conceptualization and remediation of serious psychiatric illness. None the less, the vast majority of outpatients with whom I work do not suffer from chemical depressions, broken brains or genetic abnormalities. For these clients, offering a pill is offering a medical misattribution, an iatrogenic resistance to examining their lives and psyches. And this can be a very dangerous development. In the words of George Miller, 'Let them have the decade of the brain. We have the century of the mind!'

w.d.   Are there other clinical 'megatrends' you foresee?

j.n.   My reading of the literature and my editing the centennial issue of *Psychotherapy*, which celebrates 100 years of American psychology (1892–1992), had led to several candidates for superordinate trends. These megatrends, for the sake of simplicity, go by the labels of Contextualism and Pluralism.

Contextualism refers to heightened sensitivity to the economic, social and political forces shaping the parameters of psychotherapy. We have relearned that contextless is meaningless. Psychotherapy cannot be conducted in a vacuum; we cannot avoid the noisy yammerings of the secular world as we have in the past. Philip Cushman (1990) convincingly warns against the peculiarly American idea of 'decontextualized' psychotherapy.

In practice, contextualism translates into creating more responsive models of mental health practice that fit into, not fight against, the rapidly changing conditions of culture. Harsh economic realities, such as stringent limitations on reimbursement, will escalate the trend toward brief, focal therapy. In theory, we see the rise of family systems; in format, acceleration of self-help groups, conjoint marital and family sessions – all bringing in the larger systems. And in research, we are witnessing renewed attention to the influence on process and outcome of external factors in the life of the therapist.

Pluralism, the second megatrend I anticipate, reflects the transition from either/or dualism to multiple option relativism. This is one antecedent of psychotherapy integration: segregation to desegregation of disparate approaches, viewing alternatives as adversity to viewing them as diversity and complementarity.

Pluralism is manifesting itself in innumerable spheres: proliferation of therapy systems, growth of various psychotherapy provider groups, creative applications of a variety of research designs. Reversing a history of androcentric bias in psychotherapy, the feminist perspective, too, reflects pluralism. Beyond incisive critiques of psychotherapy as male-centred, feminists are developing new theories, methods and contexts.

w.d.   We all hear about the need for cost-efficient mental health treatments. How might this affect us by the year 2010?

j.n.   We are entering a post-industrial era, a period characterized by rapid acceleration in the rate of change. All health-care professions must adapt – or perhaps become extinct, like dinosaurs before us.

Two scenarios dominate the picture: one is of a continuing but modest shift toward more efficient, structured health care in which health maintenance organizations (HMOs), preferred provider organizations (PPOs) and employee assistance programmes (EAPs) grow at the expense of the private practices. The other scenario, outlined by Nick Cummings (1986; 1988), is more draconian.

Cummings predicts a period of severe transition during which quality of services will deteriorate since the traditional manner in which psychotherapy is delivered renders mental health professionals vulnerable to the new emphasis on health-cost containment. Psychotherapy is particularly vulnerable to disruption because insurance carriers do not regard mental health coverage as essential and because there is a glut of psychotherapists. As a result, he estimates that in 1995 most health-care delivery will be controlled by five or six giant health corporations. He also believes that 50 per cent of psychotherapists in independent practice today are unlikely to survive; those who will survive will learn the new delivery system or they will be employees of corporate health.

W.D.   How might a psychotherapy student or a clinical practitioner best prepare him or herself for the future that you just outlined?

J.N.   The lessons are probably the same, be it a survival kit for psychotherapists now in practice or a career strategy for students now in training. Let me restate that I do not necessarily endorse these shifts myself, but realism must temper my idealism.

Here's a blending of what Nicholas Cummings and I might recommend. First, abandon the concept of cure. This is part and parcel of the medical model that has little relevance to psychotherapy. Improvement and preparation for intermittent psychotherapy throughout the life cycle are the realistic goals. Second, become proficient in brief psychotherapy, at least as one treatment option you provide. Time-limited therapy has its own concepts and models, so practitioners simply cannot dehydrate long-term treatment and expect it to work as efficiently.

Something else I would advise clinicians is to learn targeted or focal interventions for specific problems. Prescriptive treatment for, say, marital discord, anxiety disorders, depression, grief reactions, chronic pain and the like would also encourage clinicians to integrate themselves into the entire field of health. Behavioural medicine is certainly in the ascendancy, and clinicians will increasingly need to evolve themselves into an integrated health resource; not only traditional psychotherapy, but also stress management, health psychology, life-style promotion. One of my specializations, in fact, is the psychological treatment of chronic pain for which there seems to be an unending source of referrals.

The next recommendation is advice I haven't taken myself – learn to market your services. Nicholas Cummings likes to say that 'marketing or morbidity' will become the practitioner's equivalent to the researcher's 'publish or perish'. In addition, concentrate on therapeutic approaches and formats destined to expand. Individual psychoanalytic therapy is not growth stock; short-term, cognitive-behavioural, conjoint formats will probably pay greater dividends.

Finally, and for me most obviously, develop into an excellent psychotherapist. Nothing succeeds like success, and I believe there will always be a place in independent practice for the best in any profession.

w.d.   You mentioned earlier that your hope for the future of psychotherapy needs to be tempered by realism. But I'm going to be a fairy godfather to you now, John, and I'm going to give you three magical wishes. If you had to improve the practice of psychotherapy around the world, what would these wishes be?

j.n.   That offer strikes me as a projective test. How do I prioritize the constituent elements of successful therapy? What three things do I value over all others? It's a challenging but welcomed opportunity and I have pondered over this one quite a bit. Here they are.

Wish No 1: Routine use of empirical research to select treatment. It's hardly a new idea. Clinicians and researchers alike have long called for the development of psychotherapy with a strong empirical base. This has at least two meanings. The first is the use of research to inform practice, as in the selection of clinical methods and relationship stances; the second is in the careful, objective evaluation of the effects of the psychotherapies.

This first wish is a direct result of my lifelong conviction that psychotherapy should be predicated primarily on client need and empirical research, and secondarily on clinician preference. I don't mean to denigrate preferences; we need to feel comfortable with our favourite methods, to be convinced of their validity and to communicate this conviction to patients. However, I do object to personal preferences dictating treatment selection when they are in stark contrast to existing clinical and research knowledge. To put it bluntly, the therapist's theoretical narcissism should not be placated at the client's expense.

Wish No 2: Deep caring and abiding respect for our clients. It seems so fundamental, so basic but it is frequently masked by our preoccupation with DSM-III-R diagnoses, case formulations, technical interventions, insurance requirements, *ad nauseum*. It may be impossible to impart or to inculcate this commitment in trainees, but I have concluded that this deep caring, this ongoing respect, is the *sine qua non* of a positive therapy experience.

Wish No 3: That one of my first two wishes would actually come true and be implemented throughout the world. You'll see to that, won't you, Windy?

W.D.   I would hope that I could do that, John. Now before we finish, I'd like to look at the future of John Norcross. One of the reasons I invited you to be interviewed is that I wanted to have somebody who had already made a contribution to the field, but that the bulk of their career was ahead of them. At age 33, you've made one hell of a contribution to the field already. How are you going to keep it up, John?

J.N.   A frightening prospect in my professional life, to be sure. After my first book, the *Handbook of Eclectic Psychotherapy* (Norcross 1986), became a professional bestseller as a result of being selected as the main selection by most of the psychotherapy book clubs, one of my brothers asked me, 'How are you going to top that?' I pondered his question for quite awhile. Perhaps I can match it, but one of the dangers of being an early success is the neurotic pressure of feeling one should top each and every earlier success. It's not an entirely new experience for me; for example I'm still known, both affectionately and pejoratively, as the 'baby' of my clinical doctoral programme since I was the youngest admitted.

However, I remind myself that success is a journey, not a destination. I love exactly what I'm doing and I don't spend a lot of time worrying about my future accomplishments until a well-intentioned interviewer provokes the anxiety in me.

In broader terms, I hope the future will bring more of the same. I'm enthusiastic about my chosen profession of clinical psychology. It sounds corny, but I hope to continue to advance the science of psychotherapy and to promote human development. The hectic balance among academic, clinical and editorial responsibilities has been quite gratifying.

I foresee trying to work in two directions. One is to spend more time with my family and friends, although I've been pledging this for three years now with only minimal success to date. The second is, perhaps, to direct a clinical doctoral programme, to put my ambitious training sequence and training evaluation ideas into practice. But then I'll experience the disadvantage of increased administrative and committee work, which I truly despise. I'll have to make a decision about that at some point.

All in all, I'm pleased with where I am and who I am. I try not to become complacent, but I relish my family and my work. Freud foretold it many years ago: the meaning of life is *leiben und arbeiten* (to love and to work).

w.d.   And I wish you all the best in the future, John, in pursuit of those two objectives.

j.n.   Thank you very much.

FURTHER READING

For those who wish to read further about the work of John Norcross, the following books and articles are recommended.

Psychotherapy integration

Norcross, J. C. and Grencavage, L. M. (1989) Eclecticism and integration in psychotherapy: major themes and obstacles, *British Journal of Guidance and Counselling* 17: 227–47.

Saltzman, N. and Norcross, J. C. (eds) (1990) *Therapy Wars: Contention and Convergence in Differing Clinical Approaches*, San Francisco: Jossey-Bass.

Systematic and prescriptive eclecticism

Norcross, J. C. (ed.) (1986) *Handbook of Eclectic Psychotherapy*, New York: Brunner/Mazel.

Norcross, J. C. (1991) Prescriptive matching in psychotherapy: psychoanalysis for simple phobias?, *Psychotherapy* 28.

The person of the therapist

Norcross, J. C. and Guy, J. D. (1989) Ten therapists: the process of becoming and being, in W. Dryden and L. Spurling (eds) *On Becoming a Psychotherapist*, London: Routledge.

Norcross, J. C. and Prochaska, J. O. (1986) Psychotherapist heal thyself II: the self-initiated and therapy-facilitated change of psychological distress, *Psychotherapy* 23: 345–56.

Theoretical orientation

Norcross, J. C. (1985) In defense of theoretical orientations for clinicians, *The Clinical Psychologist* 38(1): 13–17.

Norcross, J. C. and Prochaska, J. O. (1983) Clinicians' theoretical orientations: selection, utilization, and efficacy, *Professional Psychology* 14: 197–208.

Personal therapy

Norcross, J. C. and Prochaska, J. O. (1984) Where do behavior (and other) therapists take their troubles? II, *Behavior Therapist* 7: 26–7.
Norcross, J. C., Strausser, D. J. and Faltus, F. J. (1988) The therapist's therapist, *American Journal of Psychotherapy*, 42: 53–66.

Clinical training

Norcross, J. C., Beutler, L. E. and Clarkin, J. F. (1990). Training in differential treatment selection, in *Systematic Treatment Selection: Toward Targeted Therapeutic Interventions*, New York: Brunner/Mazel.
Stevenson, J. F. and Norcross, J. C. (1987) Current status of training evaluation in clinical psychology, in B. Edelstein and E. Berler (eds) *Evaluation and Accountability in Clinical Training*, New York: Plenum.

Self-change

Norcross, J. C., Prochaska, J. O. and DiClemente, C. C. (1986) Self-change of psychological distress: laypersons' vs psychologists' coping strategies, *Journal of Clinical Psychology* 42: 834–40.
Prochaska, J. O., DiClemente, C. C. and Norcross, J. C. (in press) In search of how people change: applications to addictive behavior, *American Psychologist*.

The future of psychotherapy

Norcross, J. C. (ed.) (1992) The future of psychotherapy, special issue of *Psychotherapy*.
Norcross, J. C. and Freedheim, D. K. (1991) Into the future: retrospect and prospect in psychotherapy, in D. K. Freedheim (ed.) *History of Psychotherapy*, Washington, DC: American Psychological Association.

REFERENCES

Abrams, D. B., Follick, M. J. and Biener, L. (1988) Individual versus group self-help smoking cessation at the workplace: initial impact and twelve month outcomes, in T. Glynn (Chair) *Four National Cancer Institute Funded Self-Help Smoking Cessation Trials*, Symposium presented at the annual meeting of the Association for the Advancement of Behavior Therapy, New York, November.

Alford, B. A. and Norcross, J. C. (1991) Cognitive therapy as integrative therapy, *Journal of Psychotherapy Integration* 1(3).

American Psychological Association Task Force on Education, Training, and Service in Psychology (1982) *Summary report*. Washington, DC: American Psychological Association.

Benjamin, A. (1987) *The Helping Interview*, Boston, Mass: Houghton Mifflin.

Beutler, L. E. (1983) *Eclectic Psychotherapy: A Systematic Approach*, New York: Pergamon.

Beutler, L. E. (1986) Systematic eclectic psychotherapy. In J. C. Norcross (ed.) *Handbook of Eclectic Psychotherapy*, New York: Brunner/ Mazel.

Beutler, L. E. and Clarkin, J. (1990) *Systematic Treatment Selection: Toward Targeted Therapeutic Interventions*, New York: Brunner/Mazel.

Beutler, L., Grawe, K., Mohr, D., Engle, D. and MacDonald, R. (1991) Looking for differential treatment effects: cross-cultural predictors of differential therapeutic efficacy, *Journal of Psychotherapy Integration* 1.

Beutler, L. E., Mahoney, M. J., Norcross, J. C., Prochaska, J. O., Sollod, R. M. and Robertson, M. (1987) Training integrative/eclectic psychotherapists II, *Journal of Integrative and Eclectic Psychotherapy* 6: 296–332.

Brown, B. S. (1983) The impact of political and economic changes upon mental health, *American Journal of Orthopsychiatry* 53: 583–92.

Buckley, P., Karasu, T. B. and Charles, E. (1981) Psychotherapists view their personal therapy, *Psychotherapy: Theory, Research and Practice* 18: 299–305.

Burns, D. D. (1980) *Feeling Good: The New Mood Therapy*, New York: William Morrow.

Burton, A. (ed.) (1972) *Twelve Therapists: How they Live and Actualize Themselves*, San Francisco: Jossey-Bass.

Cowen, E. L. (1982) Help is where you find it: four informal helping groups, *American Psychologist* 37: 385–95.

Cummings, N. A. (1986) The dismantling of our health system: strategies for the survival of psychological practice, *American Psychologist* 41: 426–31.

Cummings, N. A. (1988) Emergence of the mental health complex: Adaptive and maladaptive responses, *Professional Psychology: Research and Practice* 19: 308–15.

Cushman, P. (1990) Why the self is empty: toward a historically situated psychology, *American Psychologist* 45: 599–611.

Dryden, W. and Branco Vasco, A. (1991) *Dryden on Counselling, Volume 2: A Dialogue*, London: Whurr Publications.

Dryden, W. and Spurling, L. (eds) (1989) *On Becoming a Psychotherapist*, London: Routledge.

Egan, G. (1975) *The Skilled Helper: A Model for Systematic Helping and Interpersonal Relating*, Monterey, Calif: Brooks/Cole.

Ellis, A. (1987) Integrative developments in rational-emotive therapy, *Journal of Integrative and Eclectic Psychotherapy* 6: 470–9.

Frances, A., Clarkin, J. and Perry, S. (1984) *Differential Therapeutics in Psychiatry: The Art and Science of Treatment Selection*, New York: Brunner/Mazel.

Freud, S. (1900/1953) *The Interpretation of Dreams*. In *Standard Edition*. Volumes 4 and 5. London: Hogarth Press. (Original German edition 1900.)

Freud, S. (1937/1964) Analysis terminable and interminable, in J. Strachey (ed.) *Complete Psychological Works of Sigmund Freud*, London: Hogarth Press.

Goldfried, M. R. (1980) Toward the delineation of therapeutic change principles, *American Psychologist* 35: 991–9.

Goldfried, M. R. (ed.) (1982) *Converging Themes in Psychotherapy*, New York: Springer.

Goldfried, M. R. (1987) A common language for the psychotherapies: commentary, *Journal of Integrative and Eclectic Psychotherapy* 6: 200–4.

Grencavage, L. M. and Norcross, J. C. (1990) Where are the commonalities among the therapeutic common factors?, *Professional Psychology: Research and Practice* 21: 372–8.

Grunebaum, H. (1983) A study of therapist's choice of a therapist, *American Journal of Psychiatry* 140: 1,336–9.

Grunebaum, H. (1986) Harmful psychotherapy experiences, *American Journal of Psychotherapy* 40: 165–76.

Gurin, G., Veroff, J. and Feld, S. (1960) *Americans View their Mental Health*, New York: Basic Books.

Halleck, S. L. (1978) *The Treatment of Emotional Disorders*, New York: Aronson.

Harper, R. A. (1959) *Psychoanalysis and Psychotherapy: 36 Systems*, Englewood Cliffs, NJ: Prentice-Hall.

Henry, W. E., Sims, J. H. and Spray, S. L. (1971) *The Fifth Profession*:
Becoming a Psychotherapist, San Francisco: Jossey-Bass.

Henry, W. E., Sims, J. H. and Spray, S. L. (1973) *Public and Private Lives
of Psychotherapists*, San Francisco: Jossey-Bass.

Holt, R. and Luborsky, L. (1958) *Personality Patterns of Psychiatrists*, New
York: Basic Books.

Howard, G. S., Nance, D. W. and Myers, P. (1987) *Adaptive Counseling
and Therapy*, San Francisco: Jossey-Bass.

Ivey, A. E. and Authier, J. (1978) *Microcounseling* (2nd edn), Springfield,
Ill: Charles C. Thomas.

Karasu, T. B. (1986) The specificity versus nonspecificity dilemma: toward
identifying therapeutic change agents, *American Journal of Psychiatry*
143: 687–95.

Kelly, G. A. (1955) *The Psychology of Personal Constructs*, New York:
Norton.

Lazarus, A. A. (1971) Where do behavior therapists take their troubles?,
Psychological Reports 28: 349–50.

London, P. (1988) Metamorphosis in psychotherapy: slouching toward
integration, *Journal of Integrative and Eclectic Psychotherapy* 7: 3–12.

Mahoney, M. J. (1986) The tyranny of technique, *Counseling and Values*
30: 169–74.

Marlatt, G. A. and Gordon, J. R. (eds) (1985) *Relapse Prevention*:
Maintenance Strategies in Addictive Behavior Change, New York:
Guilford.

Messer, S. B. (1986) Behavioral and psychoanalytic perspectives at therapeutic choice points, *American Psychologist* 41: 1261–72.

Messer, S. B. (1987) Can the Tower of Babel be completed? A critique of the
common language proposal, *Journal of Integrative and Eclectic Psychotherapy* 6: 195–9.

Naisbitt, J. and Aburdene, P. (1990) *Megatrends 2000*, New York: William
Morrow.

Norcross, J. C. (1985) In defense of theoretical orientations for clinicians,
The Clinical Psychologist 38(1): 13–17.

Norcross, J. C. (ed.) (1986) *Handbook of Eclectic Psychotherapy*, New York:
Brunner/Mazel.

Norcross, J. C. (ed.) (1987) *Casebook of Eclectic Psychotherapy*, New York:
Brunner/Mazel.

Norcross, J. C. (1988a) Response to Wolpe, *American Journal of Psychotherapy* 42: 509–10.

Norcross, J. C. (1988b) Supervision of integrative psychotherapy, *Journal of
Integrative and Eclectic Psychotherapy* 7: 157–66.

Norcross, J. C. (1990a) Commentary: eclecticism misrepresented and
integration misunderstood, *Psychotherapy* 27: 297–300.

Norcross, J. C. (1990b) Personal therapy for psychotherapists: one solution,
Psychotherapy in Private Practice 8: 45–59.

Norcross, J. C. (1991) Prescriptive matching in psychotherapy: psychoanalysis for simple phobias?, *Psychotherapy* 28.

Norcross, J. C. (ed.) (1992) The future of psychotherapy, special issue of *Psychotherapy*.

Norcross, J. C., Alford, B. A. and DeMichele, J. T. (in press) The future of psychotherapy: Delphi data and concluding observations, *Psychotherapy*.

Norcross, J. C., Beutler, L. E. and Clarkin, J. F. (1990) Training in differential treatment selection, in *Systematic Treatment Selection: Toward Targeted Therapeutic Interventions*, New York: Brunner/Mazel.

Norcross, J. C. and Goldfried, M. R. (eds) (in preparation) *Handbook of Psychotherapy Integration*, New York: Basic Books.

Norcross, J. C. and Grencavage, L. M. (1989) Eclecticism and integration in psychotherapy: major themes and obstacles, *British Journal of Guidance and Counselling* 17: 227–47.

Norcross, J. C. and Guy, J. D. (1989) Ten therapists: the process of becoming and being, in W. Dryden and L. Spurling (eds) *On Becoming a Psychotherapist*, London: Routledge.

Norcross, J. C. and Napolitano, G. (1986) Defining our Journal and ourselves, *International Journal of Eclectic Psychotherapy* 5: 249–55.

Norcross, J. C. and Prochaska, J. O. (1983) Clinicians' theoretical orientations: selection, utilization, and efficacy, *Professional Psychology* 14: 197–208.

Norcross, J. C. and Prochaska, J. O. (1986a) Psychotherapist heal thyself I: the psychological distress and self-change of psychologists, counselors, and laypersons, *Psychotherapy* 23: 102–14.

Norcross, J. C. and Prochaska, J. O. (1986b) Psychotherapist heal thyself II: the self-initiated and therapy-facilitated change of psychological distress, *Psychotherapy* 23: 345–56.

Norcross, J. C. and Prochaska, J. O. (1988) A study of eclectic (and integrative) views revisited, *Professional Psychology: Research and Practice* 19: 170–4.

Norcross, J. C., Prochaska, J. O. and Hambrecht, M. (1991) Treating ourselves vs. treating our clients: a replication with alcohol abuse, *Journal of Substance Abuse*, 3: 123–9.

Norcross, J. C., Ratzin, A. C. and Payne, D. (1989) Ringing in the New Year: the change processes and reported outcomes of resolutions, *Addictive Behaviors* 14: 205–12.

Norcross, J. C. and Stevenson, J. F. (1984) How shall we judge ourselves? Training evaluation in clinical psychology programs, *Professional Psychology: Research and Practice* 15: 497–508.

Norcross, J. C., Strausser, D. J. and Faltus, F. J. (1988) The therapist's therapist, *American Journal of Psychotherapy* 42: 53–66.

Norcross, J. C., Strausser, D. J. and Missar, C. D. (1988) The processes and outcomes of psychotherapists' personal treatment experiences, *Psychotherapy* 25: 36–43.

Norcross, J. C. and Thomas, B. L. (1988) What's stopping us now? Obstacles to psychotherapy integration, *Journal of Integrative and Eclectic Psychotherapy* 7: 74–80.

Patterson, C. H. (1989) Eclecticism in psychotherapy: is integration possible?, *Psychotherapy* 26: 157–61.

Paul, G. L. (1967) Strategy of outcome research in psychotherapy, *Journal of Consulting Psychology* 31: 109–19.

Perry, W. (1970) *Forms of Intellectual and Ethical Development in the College Years: A Scheme*, New York: Holt, Rinehart & Winston.

Prochaska, J. O. (1984) *Systems of Psychotherapy: A Transtheoretical Analysis* (2nd edn), Homewood, Ill: Dorsey Press.

Prochaska, J. O. and DiClemente, C. C. (1984) *The Transtheoretical Approach: Crossing the Traditional Boundaries of Therapy*, Homewood, Ill: Dow Jones-Irvin.

Prochaska, J. O. and DiClemente, C. C. (1986) The transtheoretical approach, in J. C. Norcross (ed.) *Handbook of Eclectic Psychotherapy*, New York: Brunner/Mazel.

Prochaska, J. O. and Norcross, J. C. (1982) The future of psychotherapy: a Delphi poll, *Professional Psychology* 13: 620–7.

Prochaska, J. O. and Norcross, J. C. (1983) Psychotherapists' perspectives on treating themselves and their clients for psychic distress, *Professional Psychology: Research and Practice* 14: 642–55.

Ricks, D. F. (1974) Supershrink: methods of a therapist judged successful on the basis of adult outcomes of adolescent patients, in D. F. Ricks, M. Roff and A. Thomas (eds) *Life History Research in Psychopathology*, Minneapolis, Minn: University of Minnesota Press.

Riebel, L. K. (1982) Theory as self-portrait and the ideal of objectivity, *Journal of Humanistic Psychology* 22: 91–110.

Robertson, M. (1979) Some observations from an eclectic therapist, *Psychotherapy: Theory, Research and Practice* 16: 18–21.

Robertson, M. (1984) Teaching psychotherapy in an academic setting, *Psychotherapy* 21: 209–12.

Rotter, J. B. (1954) *Social Learning Theory and Clinical Psychology*, Englewood Cliffs, NJ: Prentice-Hall.

Saltzman, N. and Norcross, J. C. (eds) (1990) *Therapy Wars: Contention and Convergence in Differing Clinical Approaches*, San Francisco: Jossey-Bass.

Silverman, L. H. (1976) Psychoanalytic theory: the reports of my death are greatly exaggerated, *American Psychologist* 31: 621–37.

Skinner, B. F. (1986) What is wrong with daily life in the western world?, *American Psychologist* 41: 568–74.

Sloane, R. B., Staples, F. R., Cristol, A. H., Yorkson, N. J. and Whipple, K. (1975) *Short-Term Analytically Oriented Psychotherapy Versus Behavior Therapy*, Cambridge, Mass: Harvard University Press.

Stevenson, J. F., Norcross, J. C., King, J. T. and Tobin, K. G. (1984) Evaluating clinical training programs: a formative effort, *Professional Psychology: Research and Practice* 15: 218–29.

Stevenson, J. F. and Norcross, J. C. (1985) Evaluation activity in psychology training clinics: national survey findings, *Professional Psychology: Research and Practice* 16: 29–41.

Stevenson, J. F. and Norcross, J. C. (1987) Current status of training evaluation in clinical psychology, in B. Edelstein and E. Berler (eds) *Evaluation and Accountability in Clinical Training*, New York: Plenum.

Stiles, W. B., Shapiro, D. A. and Elliott, R. (1986) Are all psychotherapies equivalent?, *American Psychologist* 41: 165–80.

Strupp, H. H. (1975) Training the complete clinician, *The Clinical Psychologist* 28(4): 1–2.

Strupp, H. H. (1982) The outcome problem in psychotherapy: contemporary perspectives, in J. H. Harvey and M. M. Parks (eds) *Master Lecture Series*, vol. 1, Washington, DC: American Psychological Association.

Strupp, H. H. (1986) The nonspecific hypothesis of therapeutic effectiveness: a current assessment, *American Journal of Orthopsychiatry* 56: 513–20.

Taylor, S. E. (1983) Adjustment to threatening events: a theory of cognitive adaptation, *American Psychologist* 38: 1161–73.

Veroff, J., Douvan, E. and Kulka, R. A. (1981a) *The Inner America*, New York: Basic Books.

Veroff, J., Douvan, E. and Kulka, R. A. (1981b) *Mental Health in America*, New York: Basic Books.

Wachtel, P. L. (1977) *Psychoanalysis and Behavior Therapy: Toward an Integration*, New York: Basic Books.

Wachtel, P. L. (1987) *Action and Insight*, New York: Guilford Press.

Wampler, L. D. and Strupp, H. H. (1976) Personal therapy for students in clinical psychology: a matter of faith? *Professional Psychology* 7: 195–201.

Wedding, D. and Corsini, R. J. (eds) (1989) *Case Studies in Psychotherapy*, Itasca, Ill: Peacock.

Wogan, M. and Norcross, J. C. (1982) Sauce for the goose: a response to Wolpe, *American Psychologist* 37: 100–2.

Wolfe, B. E. and Goldfried, M. R. (1988) Research on psychotherapy integration: recommendations and conclusions from an NIMH workshop, *Journal of Consulting and Clinical Psychology* 56: 448–51.

Wolpe, J. (1981) Behavior therapy versus psychoanalysis: therapeutic and social implications, *American Psychologist* 36: 159–64.

Wolpe, J. (1988) Letter to the editor, *American Journal of Psychotherapy* 42: 509.

INDEX

Entries accompanied by '(JCN)' refer specifically to discussions of John Norcross's personal experience in relation to the indexed subject.